Jesus Gives Life

Jesus Gives Life

**The story
of a completely normal
city slicker**

Gitta Tost

Translation into English: Nardina Alongi

Bibliographical information from the German National Library:
The German National Library lists this publication in the German National Bibliography, detailed bibliographical data is available on the Internet at http://dnb.dnb.de

© 2019
Produced and published by: BoD – Books on Demand, Norderstedt.
ISBN: 9783748120582

Contents

Looking back at the past

Most people only write their memoires at the end of their earthbound lives, which is perfectly understandable. Mine are a bit different. I was only 42 when I wrote my first book, which amongst other things included a brief outline of my life up to then. At that time I had no intention of writing a follow-up to this book, especially as only ten years have passed since then. The situation seems unusual to many people, but what has happend in my life since 27.11.2011 is also not easy to explain. To cut a long story short, that was the day I turned to Jesus. In other words, I've been a born-again Christian ever since. I would now like to take you on a journey through the first few years of my new life and I hope that reading this might just get one or two of you thinking. The title of this book might surprise some readers, but there's a very simple explanation. I started working as a writer in 2008. I was doing a lot of walking back then, which was a new experience for me. The result was that I was able to write down the things I realised then as I was hiking around the highlands and the uplands. The title of the book that came out in 2010 was "From A Couch Potato to a Dedicated Hiker, The Story of a Completely Normal City Slicker". At that time I was mainly interested in showing that anyone can get motivated to become active without spending very much so they can feel better both physically and mentally. This is because hiking is one of nicest leisure activities I know. You don't need any special skills or talents even if you're covering a longer distance in the great outdoors. For me, the aim of any hike is to confirm for myself that I have achieved something. And lots of people who have also recently discovered this hobby themselves, or who have always loved nature, will agree with me on this point. But as I said, in this book I also described the life I led as a young person and later as an adult in two different social systems.

Another one of my books appeared on the market about a year later, in which I wrote about all the things I have experienced as I was travelling in 2009. This one year was particularly important for me, because I was able to make four trips abroad in such a short space of time. In some cases, the things I realised on my travels even changed how I see the world. In Denmark, Egypt, South Africa and in the USA I was able to forge contacts with the people living there and get to know their way of life and culture a little better. With the differences between the countries, the views of the people who live in them are equally different. Once the second book, the "Concise Story of a Globetrotter, Travelog of a Quite Common City

Slicker" had been published in 2011, the English version of the book came onto the market a year later. This was then followed by a creative break, because I had a lot of catching up to do as someone who had recently become a Christian. I wanted to study the Bible so I devoured a lot of secondary literature to help me understand the Bible. And I swore to myself that I would only write another book when someone asked me to. I had actually had the idea for a new book for a while. I wanted to write about my experiences, but I kept on pushing this plan back. But I did put up a lot of Facebook posts, because I wanted to share the things I had realised with the people around me. Since 2015 I've also had the page "Jesus gibt Leben" (Jesus Gives Life) on Facebook. I collect donations for an orphanage in Cameroon on there. With this it's just astonishing how much Jesus has also got involved in my life, because of course the idea for this project did not just come from me. That's the reason I gave the book this title.

In May 2014 someone did actually ask me if I wanted to write a book for him to publish. There were various reasons why the manuscript was not published initially. But I did start writing again. In this book I would now like to tell you what happened in the first seven years of my new life as someone who had become a Christian. Perhaps with the help of my story, one or two people might recognise what happens to someone who devotes their heart and soul to God. Anyone who has turned to Christ is actually a new person and this starts a gradual but positive change for the better in nearly every case. People tell the most amazing stories, in which they acknowledge how much Jesus has transformed their lives. Criminals have even become pastors and drug addicts have become social workers, because these people, who are human beings just like us, are particularly good at recognising the situation that other people who have lost their way are in and showing them how they can escape from misery and despair. God particlulary loves to take unto Himself those who are disadvantage by life. It is even more interesting when people who have made it their job to campaign against Christians eventually recognise the truth because of cetain events in their life and later become a follower of Christ and preach the Gospel themselves. They bring to life the story of Paul the Apostle. For me personally, these facts and the hope that many more people will convert to Jesus are the motivation for me to face God's worst enemies. Proving the existence of our Creator is impossible, because He wants us to find our way to Him through faith alone. It would be easy for God to prove his existence by supernatural miracles. But this would lead to some people only accepting him as their Lord out of fear. But what God wants is for us to come to Him on our own initiative, because of a deeply held conviction and love. My own story is not as spectacular, but it might be worth taking a little look behind the scenes to see the only truth at the end of the day, which is that God loves us and wants nothing more than for every human being to be saved. As far as I'm concerned, I've pretty much always been a happy and content human being. God has given me everything I need to lead a full life. He has even blessed me beyond measure because I basically possess everything that an earthly being could ever wish for. I would be happy if I could pass on some of my joy, gratitude and contentment and if I could use these lines to pull some people out of their indifference by giving them hope.

Anyone who has read my first book knows that I grew up in Marienberg, a small town in the Ore Mountains. Whilst my parents were God-fearing people, their faith had its limits. In our town churchgoers like my parents were often jokingly referred to as "U-boat Christians", because they only turned up at church twice a year, at Easter and at Christmas. I am still firmly convinced that they both believed in God and showed Him the respect He deserves. But they never managed to teach us children the true faith, because they never got to know God personally during their earthly existence. In other words, they were not born-again Christians. For my sister and for me, it was often not easy to maintain a good relationship with God. As children we were always outsiders, because we had to go to church and of course at the time we felt that this was something we were being forced to do. Even in the Protestant town of Marienberg there were few believers and even fewer people who had found Christ. Being forced to do something soon leads to rejection. That is definitely one of the reasons why my sister doesn't want to have anything else to do with God today. What's also important is the fact that we grew up under Socialism. However, whilst the church was sort of tolerated at that time, basically anyone who believed in God and declared this openly was labelled as an ignorant simpleton and subjected to ridicule and pity. Some devout Christians even had massive problems, because they were denied a place at university for example. Most citizens of East Germany were atheists, because it just made life easier. In schools and throughout the educational system, a view of the world that rejected God was systematically developed and taught, which regards all scientific achievements and advances as the result of human intelligence that has grown up over the years. There was no place for God in many people's minds, because then they would have had to admit that there really is a Creator, who has control over everything that happens to us and around us. Human beings would no longer be at the centre of everything that happens. Personally, I always had the feeling that some people were scared that we would then be worth less, even as the most intelligent creatures on the planet. In the Age of Science, many of my "modern and progressive" fellow citizens claim that humanity has created the enormous leap forward in every field of science we know over the last few hundred years using its own initiative and with the potential to find things out it has acquired itself. There is no longer any space for stories full of miracles, like those that can be found in the Bible. The most that anyone then believes is that Jesus Christ actually lived on this Earth and helped people.

I should also add that some of my thoughts were also very similar up until the day of my conversion. I had no idea how all of the miracles in the Bible could have actually happened. From a human perspective, a lot of things are just not possible. Many people think: "Miracles are not in fashion any more and contradict the things we know today that are based on science." But we just cannot forget that nothing is impossible for God. He is the spirit that created everything out of nothing. None of us would exist without God, let alone have feelings like hatred and love for oneself. Some non-believers do at least admit that even today they don't have any plausible explanation for how the universe was created. But they are firmly convinced that this mystery will be solved by humanity one day. God openly shows His existence in some situations, especially in spontaneous healing. These miracles cannot be explained by the non-believers and their rational thinking either, but they would not admit to the world that only God is capable of doing anything like this however much you paid them. The Lord does not reveal Himself to everyone in the same way. He chooses the people He wants to trust or those He wants to share knowledge with. The Creator would never prove to an atheist that He actually exists. First of all, He doesn't need to do that and secondly God would never support someone who mocks Him. I also used to find it hard to describe God, because I didn't know how I was supposed to define His existence. Accepting a spirit as real is not easy, if it can't be perceived with the human senses. Most people are made up of a well developed body and a soul, which they use to perceive a wide variety of sensations. However, God's Holy Spirit is the big difference and this affects everyone differently. God looks into people's hearts and knows precisely how they're feeling and what they're thinking. If He notices that someone is trying to get close to

Him, then He will find a way to reach them. I would never have talked so freely about our Creator, even just a few years ago, because I was always scared of being labelled as an idiot. But I hadn't turned to Christ then either. God works in everyone, but people don't often want to accept this. You only have to think about how often life has changed by chance in a way that you were not expecting. And if you then reflect on this and understand that this coincidence was just you being steered in the right direction, then you can get an idea of how God works. Even people who have turned to crime as a result of terrible circumstances in their lives can feel a small part of God's presence. They know precisely when they're doing something wrong, because their conscience tries to stop them. But the less they are bothered by a bad conscience, the less influence God has on these people. I have been thinking about these sorts of things a lot over the last few years, because at the end of the day I would like to understand how God is a positive influence on our own lives. As I did this I remembered lots of little indicents that I found very strange when they happened, but which I dismissed as lucky breaks at the time.

I think the story of our trip to Denmark in 1992 is pretty weird. We wanted to spend the New Year with friends there, so we set of from Magdeburg in two cars and then just kept heading north on the motorway. Back then we were so wet behind the ears that we never wrote down the address of where we were staying or even had an atlas in the car, and we didn't have a satnav or a mobile then of course. That meant that we were totally reliant on our friends, who did know they way. As often happens in situations like this, we lost sight of each other a few hours later, due to the bad weather and the poor visibility. However, we were already in the middle of Denmark at the time, so we had already been on the road for over ten hours. Just as we had decided to give up and drive back to Germany, our friends appeared ten meters to our right driving their car down a hill. Things like this don't just happen, God shows people the way. Another example; my partner and I wanted to visit a friend in Hamburg. On the way there I put the address somewhere safe in the car, but then I couldn't find it when we got to the historic port. I could only remember the street she lived in. We asked the first person we bumped into as we walked along whether she knew my friend, and it was her neigbour who was on the way home, so she just told us to come with her. Later on we found out that this street is several kilometers long. So we would never have found the right address by ourselves. In this case the timing was perfect – we were in the right place at the right time.

And there's one more example; we - my partner and I – wanted to meet my parents one weekend in Rangsdorf. They had rented a bungalow there. When we arrived in the small town, we couldn't remember the name of the street the bungalow was in. To start with, I didn't think this would be much of a problem, because I thought that Rangsdorf couldn't be that big. When we got to the town and asked a man where the bungalows were, he thought we would laugh at him and would be a bit annoyed when he replied that there were more than a thousand bungalows in the town. In this case, there was basically no chance of finding the right one. We still tried and eventually met my parents, because my mum looked out of the bungalow's window at exactly the same time as we were starting a final lap around the village of bungalows, before we headed back home in failure. Another time we wanted to meet up with some friends at a lake. But again this time we didn't know exactly where their bungalow was. We then found them right on the bank of the lake, because they were just going swimming at the very moment we arrived there. With all of these incidents, don't forget that there weren't any mobile phones at the start of the nineties, so we couldn't communicate that easily if we had lost sight of each other. But of course I must also admit that we weren't very streetwise as we went through life. Another great story happended to me while I was studying abroad in Odessa. It was on the morning of one of the exam days, when all of my flatmates were pacing backwards and forwards around the room still very stressed, because they were so wound up. We had got up far too early and so I didn't know what to do with all this time I had. So I sat on my bed and quickly learnt another poem in Russian. You can imagine how astonished I was when I was asked to recite this particular poem during my exam. There were a lot of other poems to choose from. I'm sure that everyone has similar stories like this they could tell. God lending a helping hand with events is something that often happens. Lots of people then say it was a coincidence that they were in the right place at the right time. The situation only seems weird to them when the coincidences happen one after another, because nobody can really be that lucky.

I often enjoy telling my clients the story of how I ended up in my current job as a social worker. My aim when I tell it to them is to show that commitment of any kind is worthwhile and that you should just try everything to be successful. You should never give up, even if the situation you find yourself in seems hopeless, because you think that anything humanly possible you could try to get yourself out of the unfortunate position is just pointless. If God is at your side to support you, He really will find a way out for us. After I finished university I was working as a teacher in Leipzig. It wasn't the right job for me. Whilst I really liked working with young people and I loved discussing things with them even more, I didn't enjoy anything else very much. So one day I prayed to God: "Please give me a job I like, preferably a job as a social worker!" I did believe in God at that time. But I didn't actually think that He answered prayers and directly affected what people do. At the time I was a normal, sinful and not always honest person and I tended to imagine that God would judge me for this one day when I died. But I also told myself that I still had a lot of time until then and that things wouldn't be all that bad. I also comforted myself with the thought that there are a lot of people whose behaviour was much worse than mine. That's how I soothed my guilty conscience. But I still wasn't happy with the way I was acting. I would never have realised that God really exists now and always and could see my weaknesses even at that moment. This is mainly due to the fact that Christians who haven't repented, who sort of believe that God exists, but have never turned to Jesus Christ and so have not been reborn, do not have a genuine relationship with God, so they don't realise what He's doing directly either. I left Leipzig in the summer of 1995, because I wanted to start a new life in Magdeburg. Exactly six months after my prayer I got the job I had asked God for in my prayers. The timing was perfect, because the position came up just when I was still looking for a job in Magdeburg. The colleague who had been working in the service for young migrants until then moved to a different job in pregnancy counselling at the same place. The director of the local Worker's Welfare Association (AWO) in Magdeburg had to find someone to take over from her very quickly to secure continued funding for this position.

A few months earlier I had sent unsolicited applications to all of the charities in the town, applying for a job as a social worker. This wouldn't even be possible at all today, because the training I had received as a teacher was completely different. But at that there still were not enough trained social workers in the east of Germany, because these courses have only been available at university since the Berlin Wall came down. My boss had remembered that she still had my application in her desk drawer. I was well suited for this job with my qualifications. As well as this, in Leipzig I had already had a lot to do with ethnic Germans resettling back to Germany, because they were living in a home near our school. These people are the descendants of Germans who had emigrated to Russia hundreds of years ago, who today mainly come to Germany from that country or from Kazakhstan. It was also a really big advantage that I can speak Russian. Nearly all of the first few migrants who came to Magdeburg came from Eastern Europe. This meant that I was able to communicate with them very easily, which was one of the reasons we always had a lot of people coming to us for advice. And all of a sudden it became clear to me why I had studied Russian for five years. Since Germany was reunified, there were basically no more jobs for Russian teachers in the east of the country. The people had had enough of having to learn a language they didn't like for decades. But in my new job I suddenly needed it again. God can foresee every situation and already knows today what will be needed in a few years' time. That's why He made it possible for me to complete my A-levels in a roundabout way and then successfully finish university. Lots of things happened on the way there, which were little more than a surprise I barely noticed at the time. Today I know that even back then God intervened in my life very frequently to support me.

My rebirth on 27.11.2011

I have been working for the AWO as a migration advisor since 1996. Before I start talking about the day I was reborn, I'd like to go back a few years for a moment. I live in a city, which is characterised by the fact that there are hardly any Christians still living there, as a result of the forty years of re-education of people in the GDR. Of course we've had freedom of speech in this country, but Magdeburg has always been a working class town, where it definitely wasn't easy for anyone to live openly with their faith. As I said, I grew up in another area and so I was confronted with faith in God even as a child. At the end of the 1990s the Lord put me into a community that was made up entirely of non-believers. Sometimes I wonder what the point is. But perhaps He just wanted me to exert some infleunce on all of these people, so that He can use me to get them on the right track eventually. All of my relatives and friends are still non-believers today, who in some cases even massively reject any form of religion. But our tolerance always extends so far that we treat each other with respect and accept that other people have free will. My children have both been baptised, although the rest of our relatives definitely thought this was pointless. I always had a vague feeling that the Creator exerts an influence on our actions and how we live our lives. He even does this with people who will not find their faith for a few more years. Many people are now already being prepared for the task they will be given later. As a so-called Christian in name only, who describes herself as such, I only went to church at Christmas. Today I know the reason why. In all of the churches I had attended to worship up until November 2011, there was a liberal pastor preaching. These are spiritual people who are not born again Christians and who also don't believe that the Bible is the word of God. It will always be a mystery to me how someone can work in a job like this when they don't believe that Jesus sacrificed himself to save us. These people preach humanism and not the Gospel. We should have compassion for all of the creatures on this Earth and do no wrong. Whenever I hear a sermon like this, I might as well just look at the local paper. What's inside is exactly the same. These pastors have never mentioned what really matters when it comes to spreading the Gospel. I have never heard the word Hell in a sermon. The advice that we must turn to Jesus Christ if we want to receive eternal life with God is the most important message for humanity of all. So at this time I was a believer but I didn't know Christ. I felt the same way as my parents, who had never heard of the need to be born again, if you want to spend eternity in Heaven. But even so, I am still fairly sure that they are both now with God, as they died at quite a young age but always led a God-fearing life on Earth.

However, my conversion and the preparation for it were a miracle from God. One day a stranger appeared in my office. He was looking for a friend who was a foreigner, although it was not someone I knew. This young mean introduced himself like this: "My name is Robert. I am a teacher and a missionary." I found this openness very impressive. I wondered what could motivate someone to be so at ease with his faith. He just couldn't have known anything about the person he was meeting. I could have just as easily been someone who rejects God. My curiosity was aroused, and I chatted with this young man for a while longer. Normally that's as far as things would have gone with this one meeting, but God's plans often seem different from what we imagine. One of the services we offer young people at our migration centre is learning German. At the time a student was teaching the young migrants. On exactly the same day that Robert had left his visiting card behind, the teacher informed us that he was moving to Berlin. Freelance staff can terminate their working relationship at any time and without stating any reasons. But this left my colleague and me with the problem of finding a replacement teacher overnight. This person needed to be suitable for the role and have the right qualifications. But they would only get a small payment for this challenging work, because our budget is very limited. My colleague was at a loss, but I remembered the young man who had left his visiting card behind. I wrote Robert an e-mail the same day and asked him to come in for a chat. He did actualy appear and so our situation was saved. But what I hadn't realised at the time was that this young man would turn my whole life upside down. God had sent him to me, because He has plans for me, which even go as far as writing this book. Before I was born again I would never have thought about helping others find their faith, but today the situation is completely different.

Robert worked with us as a teacher for the next two years and we often got the opportiunity to have a chat. What most impressed me was that this young man had an appropriate answer ready to any question relating to faith in God. Even today I have the feeling that he knows the whole Bible inside out. He always argues so precisely that I just had to believe him. And after every time we had a chat together, I felt relieved and free inside myself. At the same time the Holy Spirit was already affecting me and it brought me the inner peace I needed and which I had always been looking for. When Robert told me that he was in personal contact with God, I initially couldn't accept this. But the more he told me about himself and his life, the more believable everything appeared to me. He was also the person who told me that we need to turn to Christ during our lifetime, unless we want to end up in eternal damnation. Even though his arguments were so accurate and effective and he was eventually able to convince me, it took two whole years before I made the decision to convert. The young man told me that God also talks to us through other people and that he sometimes surprises himself with how well he knows the Bible. Then one day something strange happened. Robert was sat at this teacher's desk preparing for his lessons. I immediately noticed that something was getting him down a bit and that he was unhappy. That just wasn't like him, because he always exuded a great deal of zest for life. Obviously I asked him what the matter was. He told me that he wanted to ask his future wife's family in Lituania if he could marry her. But he didn't have enough money, because he was still waiting for a payment he was owed. Completely spontaneously I offered to lend him six hundred Euros, which was twice what he needed. Even today I can't say why I did it. The words just came out like that, because the decision just seemed to be right to me. I just knew that I would get the money back. So I found the money and Robert later said: "When I prayed to God this morning, he told me that I shouldn't worry about the money. I would get more than I need. And I shouldn't ask anyone for the money." That's exactly what happened, and that's exactly how God is at work in people's lives. Robert had to leave us after two years, because he went to study abroad in Poland. But that was precisely the moment when I was ready to give my life to God. The timing was perfect here too. It was on a Sunday when I was sat alone in our living room. The children were already in bed and my partner wasn't home. I was on my laptop and was a bit depressed, because I wasn't that satisfied with my life. Things weren't going brilliantly at work, because we weren't getting as many clients as we wanted. I was just about to watch a video on YouTube, which had some rather dubious content, when out of nowhere a video suggestion appeared on the right, which included a woman explaining how she found her way to God. This was clearly one of God's many miracles, because I had never entered anything to do with faith under the search terms. So logically speaking this video should never have appeared. But I was curious and so I watched the short film. I was so fascinated by the stories from the lives of people who had recently become Christians that I watched at least five other similar films that evening. In each of them somebody explained their own personal experiences and how their specific circumstances had led to them turning to Jesus. At the end of the film the text of a prayer appeared, which you could use to commit yourself to Jesus. I was afraid that nothing about me would reveal itself or change at all if I said this devotional prayer. But I did say it in the end, because I thought that I would have nothing to lose. I just read it out: "Dear God, I regret all of the many sins I have committed, consciously and unconsciouly. I would like to start a new life with Jesus at my side and so I gratefully accept the sacrifice you made for use." I couldn't feel any immediate change. I just noticed that I became really calm, balanced and contented inside myself. I suddenly realized how many times I had sinned in my life. I never thought I'd ever be so sorry for anything.

I went to bed straight afterwards and that night was the only time Jesus spoke to me in a dream. Despite my joy about this change, I was scared, uncertain and depressed, because I was now the only person for miles around who had gone down this route. I asked Jesus what good any of this was if I just ended up being alone. His reply was that I shouldn't worry. Everything would be fine and would happen at the right time. I should just carry on doing the same things I had been doing and do things like tell others about myself and my new experiences on the Internet. I was able to sleep peacefully that night, but the following day I started researching things in the Bible and finding out information about the Word of God in other books. I had never read the Bible before, basically because I had never understood what it contained. I had also told Robert this, but he just said that the Holy Spirit would help me explore this book. That's exactly what happened. Today I understand most of it. It's amazing when I think about what my first steps into this new life looked like. The first thing that occurred to me was that the Holy Spirit was actually at work within me. I was suddenly able to do things that had previously seemed impossible to accomplish. Even today there are so many situations, especially in my job, where you don't know any way out and you just have to give up. But the Holy Spirit shows me what I need to do. It's just amazing. I had even more help right at the beginning. In my faith I was just like a little baby that can't do anything by itself. I was no longer able to sign anything or fill something in that wasn't the truth. Before, I had no major issue with putting a cross in the wrong place. Everyone did it after all. But now I just couldn't move my hand if I wanted to do something like that. Exactly the same thing happened with driving the car. It was just impossible to exceed the indicated speed limit. I could put my foot down as much as I wanted, but the car would not accelerate. That was all very mysterious, but it did help me a lot, especially at the start.

I have been a born again Christian since 27.11.2011 and as such I also try to convince other people to go down this route every day. God is not a mythical being, He really does exist and helps those who believe in Him. There have been too many situations to mention where I have been helped directly. I feel the Holy Spirit at work in little things nearly every day. But of course I will only write about the most remarkable cases, because otherwise the book would go on forever. Converting to God is nothing more than returning to God. And the Lord rewards this step by making life more pleasant for us right now. Of course a born again Christian can still get ill or is also not immune from committing sins. We carry this burden around with us for our whole lives, but born again Christians normally no longer want to do anything bad at all. Sometimes I really notice how my heart could just overflow with love. People that I had previously rejected are suddenly important to me. And I do things that would be inconceivable for a non-believer. But it is not through deeds that we become righteous before God, and that is why I will not boast about what has happened to me. I am telling these stories so that we all learn to believe in miracles again. So this book is not mainly about me, but about fellow human beings, whose fate has turned to good by the influence of God and also indirectly by the change in my life. Someone said to me once that even the richest people, who can afford any material possessions, will ultimately not lead a fulfilled life because they do not have inner balance. They strive more and more for the satisfaction of worldly needs and yet cannot find peace because these things are no substitute for the love of God. Anyone who has God in their heart will just feel happy and content. If this is also your aim in life, if you wish for nothing more than to finally feel peace in your heart, then read this little book! Perhaps it will even open up new perspectives for you for the rest of your life.

Swetlana's Good Fortune

Right after my conversion I wanted to share the things I had just realised with other people. I immediately started telling everyone how important it is to turn to God during our lifetime so that we can receive eternal life. Anyone who turns away from their previous life, repents their sins before God and accepts the sacrifice that Jesus made for us will already have a fulfilled life here on Earth. I don't know what exactly that looks like in other countries, but that applies to Germany one hundred percent, because in our country Christians are not persecuted and killed on account of their faith in Jesus. Of course it's incredibly difficult to convince people about the good news if they have not previously come into contact with the Gospel and have received a completely different religious or anti-religious upbringing. Up to now I have only been able to reach a few people, even though I write posts on Facebook every day about the experiences I am able to have through the Holy Spirit, which is now active within me. In the initial period of my new life I mainly wanted to get in contact with people just like me, to stop me being alone in my faith. So I fervently started looking for a community in which the Holy Spirit is present. For the first time in years I went back to church on a Sunday, specifically to my local parish church. During the service I noticed that something wasn't right. The Holy Spirit was not amongst us. There could only be one reason for this, which was that we had a liberal pastor, who is not a born again Christian and probably doesn't believe in the truth of the Bible either. Up to that moment I would never have thought this was possible. But it really is the case that various pastors are in this profession and preach pure humanism in their parishes. For them humanity is at the centre of everything and not God, our Creator. One of the things that you can recognise these pastors by is the fact that their congregations are shrinking. How can I inspire someone to accept God if I don't even believe in Him myself? And the most important job a pastor has is to win people over to the Gospel. God then showed me where I should go to church. I had remembered that the parents of a young migrant came to my office looking for help a few years ago. They are members of the congregation at the Baptist Free Church. I now went to this church and experienced what happens in a service in which you can feel the presence of the Holy Spirit. There were about 200 Christians gathered there. I found myself a seat on the end of a row of chairs roughly in the middle of the large room at the church. Just before the service started, a woman asked me whether the three seats next to me were free. I didn't look up, but just answered yes. This Christian woman and her two children squeezed past me and sat down straight away. A few seconds later the woman spoke to me, because she was totally amazed to meet me there. It was the very same person who had come to my office years before and whom I got to know personally very well in the years that followed, because we were also in touch with each other privately. That was because we both had a baby at the same time and so we then met up with each other quite a lot with our children. It later became clear that our meeting in the service was a case of divine intervention, as this woman had not been back to the church for a few months. And I have not even seen her there very often since then. Today she is not even a member of the congregation any more. What is the probability that someone I know will sit right next to me if there are still seats free everywhere and there are quite a lot of people in the room where the service is being held?

God wanted to show me that I was in the right place there. Even so, I am still unable to leave my original congregation because I was brought up in the Evangelical Lutheran tradition. The Baptist community places a great deal of emphasis on Christians making a public confession to the Father and to the congregation. A baptism is like a celebration. I don't have anything against these views, but I don't personally like being on show in front of a big group of people at all. On the other hand I do actually understand the basic principle. Jesus said that we should be baptised as a sign that we follow Him. His opinion was that we should do this as adults when we are fully aware of what we're doing so it is our own free will. The Evangelical-Lutheran Church baptises babies when they're still little, because there the view is that this means that God is protecting them completely from an early age. To be honest, as far as I'm concerned the declaration the Baptists make is more meaningful. But even so I still can't bring myself to switch congregations officially. Deep within me there is still some hope that at some point in the future lots of other congregations in Magdeburg will be reformed and the pastors will finally start doing their real work, i.e. winning people for the Gospel and increasing the community of believers. Perhaps that's just where I will be needed then. Even so, I have volunteered in the Baptist congregation for a few years. We support children with their homework and getting ready for class tests. Helping out and getting back nothing more than making shildren slightly happier gave me a feeling of satisfaction. It also made us proud whenever they were pleased about their achievements at school. We knew that we had done our bit to give these children back the desire to be successful in their education. Some of them came from dysfunctional families, where parents never take the time to address their concerns. When we spoke to them personally we were about to find out a great deal about what these little people need. Just like anyone else they also just need someone who listens to them, understands them and takes their problems seriously. Some parents really don't have it easy, if they have to look after a lot of children and always have too much to do. We hoped that some of our love would also be passed on to the children and their parents. However we ended the project in the summer of 2015, because the number of students in need had dropped, one of the maths tutors had also turned 80 and I had much less free time with my job. However, there will always be ideas for new ways of helping, and so I am also optimistic about the future as far as this is concerned.

But now it's finally time for me to talk about Swetlana, who was one of the people I took under my wing. My job as a social worker for the AWO's Youth Migration Service involves helping young migrants who have come to Magdeburg from all over the world to spend the rest of their lives here and take their first few steps in the country that is their new home. This is a very interesting job, because these young people do actually come from countries in all parts of the world and have made their way to Germany for a wide variety of reasons. In the first few years almost all of the young people I was looking after were those whose native language was Russian. That worked out very well for me, because I don't have any problems chatting with them and was able to reach out to them more easily on an emotional level. In July 2006 a man came to see me in my office, because he wasn't getting any more child benefit for his daughter Swetlana. She had just turned 18, and so the family benefits department was requesting information about what she was doing about work. As we talked it became clear that the girl had a mental disability and had just been kept at home since she arrived in Germany. The parents had never applied for financial support for the young woman or arranged anything else for her, because they came from a village in Russia where people with physical and mental disabilities did not get any funding. They are kept indoors at home there and are often looked after by their grandparents during the day. Swetlana had never gone to school in Russia and so she couldn't read or count or write. But she does speak Russian perfectly, which does indicate a certain level of mental ability.

At the time my aim was not just to explore every option for getting the family some financial support for her. I also wanted her to be integrated into society and for her to be able to work in a special workshop. I will never forget the first time we met. On a cold and wet autumn day we were stood outside the entrance to the mental health court, where we wanted to apply for the parents to get legal power of attorney for their daughter. Swetlana was just wearing slippers on her feet. I was horrified and asked her parents why she hadn't put on any outdoor shoes. Her father replied that, "She never goes out, so she doesn't need any shoes." So Swetlana had never even had her own shoes up to then and had also only rarely left their flat. She was very timid and was scared to look at me. There then followed a process that took months, but at the end of it the young woman was able to take her first few steps towards leading an independent life. Since then she has been going to the workshop for people with disabilities. Initially she found it very hard to adapt to the new situation. She just wasn't used to having so many people around her. From a purley linguistic point of view, she also couldn't understand the others. Swetlana really did have massive problems at the start, but it became easier for her as the weeks went by and in the end she got used to being picked up from home every morning and being taken to work. She really enjoyed her work, which is why she eventually preferred spending time at work to staying at home. And there was a very simple reason for this. Both of her parents are alcoholics. In the beginning they were still very much on top of things, but their condition got worse as the months went by. Today they aren't even able to hold down a job. This was an awful time for Swetlana. By this point she had come to trust me so much that she confided in me with her concerns. The young woman told me more and more frequently that she wanted to move out of her parents' flat. The problem was that her parents had to give permission for this. But they didn't want to lose the money they were now getting for their daughter and which they often spent on alcohol. At one point, when things were going really badly with her parents and you could barely have a conversation with them each day, one of my colleagues from the disability workshop gave me a good piece of advice. She said, "The best chance Swetlana has is if she can get someone else to look after her. But that just won't happen, because her parents won't give up this responsibility." To be fair to her parents I should say that they were actually worried about their daughter. But by then the alcohol had already destroyed so much that they couldn't even make clear decisions any more. I persuaded Swetlana's parents to transfer the legal power of attorney to me. They agreed, because they knew that I would never hurt them. That's why I took over the responsibility for Swetlana's care, even though I knew that this would entail more work. Before my conversion I had tried to find Swetlana a place in sheltered accommodation several times without success. There is so much demand for these rare places that there are long waiting lists. It also helped a bit that I mentioned how urgent it was. Swetlana's application disappeared somewhere amongst the huge pile. One day in November 2011 I got a call from a woman asking if we could have a meeting together. She is the legal representative of a young man who also goes to the workshop and was Swetlana's boyfriend at the time. He gave her stability whenever things were getting really bad at home again and all her parents were doing was arguing. This relationship was already a strange story, because the fact that they speak different languages meant that these two youngsters can't actually talk to each other. I met up with his carer and we discussed when and where the two of them could meet. During the conversation she told me that a place in the sheltered accommodation had just become free. I was surprised that I hadn't heard anything about this from the people who were responsible for this, but I rang them immediately. My inquiry got a pretty furious reaction from the woman who worked there. She told me that the young man's carer shouldn't actually have given me this information. But she promised me that she would consider Swetlana when the place was reallocated. Today I know that she never intended to do this.

A few weeks went by and nothing happened. So I had already given up hope. Swetlana's parents had an appointment at the job centre on one of the days following this. I wanted to go with them to be their interpreter. They didn't turn up to the appointment, because they were drunk. My reaction to this was to call them at home, to tell them that they would have to speak for themselves at the next appointment. This was a completely pointless call and normally I would never have made it either. Even today I don't know why I picked up the phone. My only explanation for any actions like this is that God is helping me directly at these moments. Swetlana was on the other end of the line. She was totally distraught and told me between her sobs that her parents were completely drunk and that she wanted to get away from them. I immediately called the lady whose job it is to allocate the flats again. It really was the perfect time. When I had rung her the first time, the free space had already been reallocated. The whole of one part of an ordinary town house had been rented for the sheltered accommodation. On every floor up the staircase there are two flats, which have accommodation for three people each. They share the bathroom and the kitchen, but everyone has their own room. A social worker is always available on the ground floor of the house during the day to take care of whatever the flatmates need. They cook together and go shopping or to concerts together. The two girls who eventually shared a flat with Swetlana until the spring of 2015 were not getting on with the woman who was actually supposed to move in there. So the woman who worked there had to find someone else to live in the flat. Well that was exactly the moment I rang her. What could be easier than not having to sift through the pile of applications, but just going for the person someone had just suggested? Swetlana got a place in the sheltered accommodation after waiting for four months - the waiting period for one of these places is normally three to four years. The carers who work in this institution were totally amazed and couldn't believe that this happened so quickly. It was something that was absolutely impossible, but just not for God. My protégée has changed so much over the last few years that there's almost nothing left to remind me of the timid little creature standing before me in her slippers in 2006.

She is a confident woman today who knows exactly what she wants. But that is also a problem for her, because she can sometimes be very stubborn too and ignores the instructions from her carers. So there were some tensions at the end of 2014. The carers in the home had a lot of conversations with her, as did I, because she kept on having arguments with her flatmates. However, in the end Swetlana eventually got her own flat in April 2015. My protégée is capable of managing all the jobs that crop up by herself, although she still can't count and so is not able to handle money. Even so she still goes shopping by herself. I'm totally amazed every time she tells me which shop she visited to buy her new clothes. She also doesn't worry about taking the tram. Her memory of the numbers depends totally on visual cues, but she does have a really good sense of direction.

She can go to the doctor by herself and can also get to other places without anyone helping. Of course Swetlana still needs to be looked after and supported in her daily life, but she does have to be a lot more independent. Unfortunately things with her parents have turned out so badly that today their own daughter no longer wants to have any contact with them. I even had to stop working with them, because they could never meet the conditions we asked them to keep and her father even stopped going to rehab. It was only at that moment that I realized that I was dependent on them. I could never say no, whenever they asked for my help, which is always a problem with alcoholics. I kept on forgiving them for their mistakes and helped them time and time again. Now that I have given up this responsibility, I can concentrate better on other cases. And Swetlana is happy with her life, because she can now even afford things from her savings. Before she never had anything left for herself from what she earnt. Today I am very pleased that I took over the legal power of attorney for her, even if this was not part of my job description. I don't personally know of any social worker in the migration service who has taken on a responsibility like this. But I don't regret my decision, because it made it possible to help this young woman find a way out of her hopeless situation and enable her to live with dignity. My respest for people with mental disabilities has also grown enormously ever since I turned to Christ. In the past I wouldn't necessarily have chosen to have anything to do with this group of people. But today I notice how much I really enjoy it whenever the people in the worskhop are pleased to see me. The way the employees there in the sheltered accommodation work with each other, which is also characterised by a great deal of trust in each other and me, is the reason that we can often solve smaller problems or sort out any difficulties very quickly. Perhaps that's also down to the fact that it's a Christian institution.

Wahid can't believe it

I'd like to tell Wahid's story, because it makes you think and probably sounds like a miracle to anyone who works as an advisor for migrants. He came to Germany from Afghanistan in 2010 as an unaccompanied minor to apply for asylum here. Although practically no citizens from this country were granted asylum at that time, they all had their own personal lawyer. These people often earn money by giving the refugees false hopes. Wahid's lawyer later once told me that she had known from the very start that his application for asylum would be rejected. And despite this she still took the money out of his pocket. Wahid was one of the first Afghan refugees I got to know. I must admit that up until then I had an image of this country in my head based on what is shown in the media. On the news and in documentaries we only see men wearing wooly caps on their heads and carrying rifles on their backs and women in a burka with a slit to see through. I'm scared of people when I can't see their face. I don't know what they're thinking and what their personal attitude to me is. You can tell both of these things from someone's facial expression. Of course, good actors can also use this to deceive me, but fortunately I've never yet had any problems with my clients. It's exactly the same with men who don't accept me because of their religion, just because I'm a woman. I didn't have a good feeling in my stomach when I was faced with my first Afghan migrant. Looking back today I can say that the things I was worried about were unjustified, at least as far as the people from this country are concerned. Nearly all of them are very hard working and are really trying hard to become integrated as quickly as possible. They have immediately reconsidered their preconceptions about what roles men and women are expected to perform, because they have noticed that they won't get anywhere in Germany if they insist on men being the ones making the decisons. After all, in Germany these people often have to seek advice from the women who work for the authorities and for official bodies.

I have also been able to observe this effect with Syrian refugees. Right from the start they are pleased that the restrictions imposed on them by the things that are not allowed in their religion are not enforced in our country and are completely meaningless. Young women in particular really do blossom. The vast majority of the young Muslims we look after actually adapt very quickly. Only a few women still turn up in their headscarves for German lessons or when they're getting advice, because they now perceive keeping their heads covered as a restriction of their freedom. The people who live strictly according to the laws of Islam don't come to us, because they seem to be afraid that we will have a negative influence on them with our democratic thinking, our liberal culture and a lifestyle where we are free to make our own decisions. This is how I see this issue, and I am just so pleased whenever I can observe what from my perspective are positive changes in the young people. Initially all Muslims seem sceptical, mainly because they're afraid of the unknown. As soon as they notice that we are nice to them and they can get help from us, then the dam is quickly broken. We have a lot of laughs and there's always a lively atmosphere in the lessons. At the start Wahid was also very reserved, shy, worried and sceptical towards everything and everyone. That was mainly due to the fact that he had to live in constant fear of being deported. When we first came into contact wth him, there was a very dedicated woman working as an intern in our migration service who really looked after him. It was very touching.

But Wahid also did quite a lot himself from the beginning, which meant that he was able to become integrated later on. He went to a training course on integrating, even though he did not get any kind of financial support as he was not a recognised refugee. His German was already perfect by the time he first came to our office. Our intern took her work very seriously and went to several barbershops with him to ask if he could do some unpaid work experience. Initially, Wahid was so reserved that he was reluctant to lift his head when people were talking to him. The manager of one of the barbershops was immediately impressed with his unassuming demeanour. Working with other institutions, we were able to make arrangements for Wahid to get work experience in this salon. The barber did not have to pay any extra costs, which meant that he was able to take him on for no additional outlay. Our young friend was thrilled from the start and even today he still does everything he can to make sure that his boss is happy with him. This first bit of work experience was followed by others and one day the manager of the salon told us that he really wanted to take Wahid on as an apprentice. At that time this shouldn't have actually been possible, because back then young people whose presence was merely tolerated in Germany were not given a permit to get a job or start an apprenticeship. Being tolerated means nothing more than the fact that the person can be deported back to their country of origin at any time, because their application for asylum has been rejected. At the time we were being told that Afghanistan was a safe country, because foreign military peacekeepers were stationed there to ensure that law and order were maintained. So Wahid would probably have been sent back to Afghanistan if he hadn't started his apprenticeship to become a barber. His boss really stood up for him, because he realised that Wahid was a hard-working member of the team, who was always available and never answered back. He even went with him twice to the Afghan Embassy in Berlin at his own expense to get him a birth certificate and a passport issued there. However, these documents were not recognised by the authorities that deal with foreigners in Germany, because the Afghan Embassy issues all its documents without checking the identity of the person. This means that there is always a reasonable doubt as to the authenticity of the information in the passport or on the birth certificate, because these are based entirely on the details provided by person who is applying for the document. His boss was very happy with him, because he was one of the best apprentices in his class. He was also so popular at the barbershop that he had already been able to build up his own list of regular customers. Of course it's easy to understand that his boss didn't want to lose him as an employee and so supported him whenever he could. Even today Wahid does not have a residence permit, because he doesn't have any documents that clearly confirm his identity. Whenever I tell this story to my colleagues at other advice centres that work with migrants, they can hardly believe it. They say that back then it was virtually impossible to start an apprenticeship for a trade if your presence in Germany was just being tolerated and if you didn't have any recognised identity papers. God also helped out here by getting involved. For the sake of full disclosure, I should explain that the situation on the labour market has improved since 2014. Today it's easier to get refugees onto an apprenticeship, even if their presence in Germany is only tolerated, because the laws about this have been relaxed. It has probably been recognised that it's better for people to start an apprenticeship than to be left to their own devices for long periods, as they are not allowed to do anything all day long. There could then be the danger of course that the young people could turn to crime out of sheer frustration. Since then, permission to start vocational training for anyone whose presence is tolerated, i.e. people who are waiting to be deported to their home country, is no longer granted if the migrant concerned cannot prove their identity. To this day I don't know what made the Foreigners' Registration Office give permission for Wahid to start his apprenticeship. In April 2015 he was even able to move into his own flat, because his employer had agreed to pay half of his rent. He was investing in this young man, because he knew that he could rely on him and that he was a very good, loyal employee.

The young people often think that I can perform miracles for them, especially if things have been going badly for months. But I don't actually do very much myself, the solutions to the problems come from God alone. So anyone who trusts in the Lord will have no need to worry. They are aware that our Creator knows us very well and would never let our lives be ruined. Today Wahid is a very confident young man, who knows exactly what he wants. The fact that he soaks up any new piece of information like a sponge is something else that I find interesting about him. He spent months following my posts on Facebook to get the lowdown on Christians. Having studied this means that today he is probably better informed than some Germans. But years of Islamic education and upbringing have left their mark. It is often very difficult for people to change the focus of their faith, even if they have recognised that they cannot always develop freely in their religion. They also hold on tightly to their faith, because it's the last link to the country they came from and their old culture. For me, Wahid is an example of how people in Germany can develop into confident, self-assured fellow citizens, if they are given the opportunity to do so. If they feel like they are a part of our society, they will not be sidelined and they will be pulling in the same direction as us Germans. My aim is to show as many young people as possible that living as a Christian without any religious pressures brings you inner peace. I think that God deliberately put me in this position, because this is where I can exert the greatest influence through my personal behaviour and, when asked, get closer to young people of other religions and tell them the good news in the Gospel. However, I will not act as a missionary, first of all because I respect every individual's free will, secondly because I work in a non-religious institution and thirdly because I'm of the opinion that missionary work is pointless anyway. That's because the person in question must realise the truth of their own accord, because it's impossible to force anyone to believe in Jesus. Some of them will definitely become Christians when they realise that this is the right way to go. I won't reach the others, but that's normal. We Christians can only tell our fellow human beings about the good news of salvation through Jesus Christ. We don't have any influence over whether or not these people eventually accept the sacrifice he made for us. The decision to turn to Christ must come from each individual. Either people open their hearts to God or they don't. God gives us all a free choice.

There have been endless numbers of questions ever since I became a Christian, to which I would love to have had the answers. At the start I couldn't understand the Bible, but lots of things seem clearer to me now that I've been studying the Holy Scriptures. There are Christians who are real role models for me in terms of enlightenment, because they can explain the Bible or who can use scientific methodology to testify that God is the only truth. These include people like Dr. Werner Gitt, Roger Liebi, John Bevere, Warren W. Wiersbe and Stephen Lonetti. I have not actually read that many books that explain faith since the 27.11.2011. But every time it was obviously the right thing to read, because I have grown and become more secure in my faith with every single book. Today I can answer questions to which my only reaction right at the start of my career as a converted Christian would have been a regretful shrug. For any of my brothers and sisters who have recently found their faith I recommend the book "A Common Theme Through the Bible" by Stephen Lonetti. There is no simpler or clearer explanation of the Christian faith.

How I made peace with Kone

When it became clear to me how terrible the fate was that awaited those people who do not confess everything to Jesus during their lifetime, I just wanted to persuade or convince everyone to end their life of sin and to follow Jesus. I'm sure you can imagine that nearly all of the people I spoke to about this didn't listen. But something else happens with people who have become Christians. They don't just serve God through their words, they also try to draw attention to themselves at the same time through positive actions. This impresses some non-believers so much that want to become followers of Jesus themselves. If we act unselflessly every day, then we are role models for our fellow citizens. Of course this isn't always successful, but the Holy Spirit is constantly helping us to do this. Loving our neighbours as much as we love ourselves is a key concept. People who are non-believers are often also helpful and friendly and also lead harmonious lives. But have they also internalized this commandment? To be honest I can't imagine this would happen at all, not least because it's something even people who have become Christians often find very hard to do. How do you think things would turn out, if one of our colleagues just complains all the time, our neighbour is the sort of person who is never satisfied and other people we know are possibly jealous of our successes and do not allow us to enjoy them? When this happens it, we find it easier to ignore these people than to talk to them. But loving them just as much as we love ourselves? From a human perspective, that's just not possible. However, God deliberately asks us to show love to our spouse, our children, our parents, our neighbours and the people we work with. If we live our lifes in this way, it sets us as Christians apart from other people. The Bible describes the good deeds we carry out every day through our love for other people as the fruit of our lives. It's virtually impossible to describe this fruit, but it does bring an incredible amount of joy. Every effort we make is worth it if we get a smile in return or even just a thank you very much. Before, I would never have thought it possible, but there's nothing that can beat happy, grateful faces looking at us full of trust. This thing I referred to as fruit stays around forever, it changes the people around us, their whole lives, their personal situation and their working environment. Love is like a viral infection, it spreads like a bushfire. And because people feel more comfortable in a situation like this, they will again and again find their way back to the loving person they met and remember the things they spoke about in confidence and the things they did together.

In contrast to this, things like fame, honour, power, money, recognition are short-lived and only bring satisfaction and joy for a limited time. What happens next once your objective has been achieved and you might possibly have got as high as you can go in your career? People who only strive for earthly success will always be dissatisfied and be looking for peace of mind. This is because striving for earthly possessions cannot satisfy this hunger. Even the richest and most successful people on this Earth are often not happy in the end, because they have already achieved the objective they set themselves. However, there must always be new, even more complicated tasks, so that they can get this feeling of satisfaction for a certain period of time. What's more, they don't often know who their real friends are and who just wants to take advantage of their money, fame and influence. We can find real happiness and balance in the little things, for example in loving our neighbour. Life is good if you can just make one person a day happy. Thoughts like this should be what motivates us. At the end of our lives, God will then ask us anyway what we achieved with the gifts he gave us like life, time, money and talents and what we did for other people. Whilst that's not entirely unimportant, it's not what motivates the things I do personally today. I don't work for a reward, I'm basically just satisfied if I can make the people around me a bit happier. That wasn't always anything like the case. I can still remember completely different times when I often got annoyed by the people I was working with, whose lack of knowledge didn't just affect themselves but other people too. In situations where there were discussions and arguments time and time again, I could become very short-tempered and had hardly any control over my negative feelings. I have one particular memory of arguing with the Coordinator of the Network for Integration and Working with Foreigners in the city of Magdeburg so much over a number of years that eventually we showed no respect to each other at all when we met. I accused him of being incompetent and so as a result he showed everyone how much he hated me.

He was basically only fighting back. And looking back today, I know that it's not my place to criticise people like that, even if I feel that I'm in the right. In any case, everyone who worked in the migration department knew that we just couldn't stand each other. I became angry whenever this man even just walked into the room. Without God's help, it would never have been possible for me to change this attitude. We would still be enemies, even today. But after I became a Christian, I felt the urgent need to make peace with this man. The main reason for this was that I still have a bad feeling today if I have a disagreement with someone. Later on I read a book about how God already knows who to put in certain key positions. We cannot always understand why certain people exert power and then abuse it. But it would certainly be asking too much for us to appreciate how everything in our lives is connected. However, it's a fact that we will be calmer and more content in ourselves, if we just accept out superiors, even if we don't like them and disagree with their decisions. We should pray for people who don't respect human rights or who just make unfair decisions that have far-reaching consequences. Even they can change their ways and eventually recognise the truth. The other stakeholders in the network could hardly believe that I had made peace with Kone of all people, when I had been his biggest enemy. I hoped that my actions would set a good example, but that's not how it turned out. Even today the relationship between the individual protagonists is icy. But even here I think that God will come up with a plan to make the situation less tense.

Ali gets a new life

The first time that Ali came to my office was in 2013, because he was in a hopeless situation. He is an Afghan by birth, but he has never been to this country, because his family emigrated to Pakistan before he was born. Things like this often happen in Islamic countries, because people who have a bit more money alway gravitate towards places where the living conditions are better. Arabic is spoken in a lot of countries in North Africa and in the Middle East, which makes the whole thing a bit easier. Ali is an intelligent young man, whose plan was to study in Pakistan. He told me his life story, which I'm repeating here without any personal opinions, because I never know how much of what people say is true. But I do believe Ali, because my impression of him is that he has always been honest. One day he is sitting in his house and hears on the radio that there has been an uprising in the city between opponents of the goverment and the militia, during which a lot of people have been injured. He wants to help and so he goes to where it was all happening. After he had been there a while doing what he could to help, the whole crowd was surrounded by the police and everyone was arrested. Anyone who was present was automatically declared to be a demonstrator and an opponent of the government. Fortunately, he was able to get away back to his house, but his name had already been registered, probably because he was seen on one of the videos that were filmed there. The police came to his house that evening to arrest him. His younger brother opened the door and when he heard from the back room that they wanted to take him away, he was able to escape across the roofs of the neighbouring houses. Since that time it has been impossible for him to live in Pakistan, because he would be arrested as soon as he arrived. Ali fled to Europe, to Sweden to be precise. The govenment there sends a lot of refugees back to their country of origin. Ali's application for asylum was rejected and he was advised to go to Afghanistan, even though he doesn't know anyone there and has never been to this country. Ali came to Magdeburg just before he was due to be deported. He was hoping that Germany would take him in.

Now of course word has got around everywhere in the world that the standard of living in our country is the highest in Europe. That is why almost every migrant who is somehow able to do so would like to come here. The result of this is that Germany is now the second most popular country for immigrants in the whole world after the USA. If you compare the two countries in terms of area alone, you can get a good idea how much pressure this puts on such a small country, which has no natural resources whatsoever and has only been able to achieve economic stability thanks to innovation in its industry. A law was passed in Dublin a few years ago to distribute migrants evenly across EU countries. This stipulated that any refugee should stay in the first European country they entered. If this provision was applied one hundred per cent of the time, a refugee would never be able to reach Germany, simply because our country is located in the middle of Europe. But Italy and Greece are supporting people in their thousands who have crossed the Mediterranean to get to Europe, by not registering them and giving them money to continue their journey to Germany. In 2014, when I took my daughter to the Hip-Hop European Championship in Rimini, I was able to see for myself how this works. These refugees always travel at night by coach, because the German authorities carry out checks on the motorways during the day. If anyone is found on one of the buses without any identity papers, that person will be in big trouble and will usually be sent back to Italy. As a result everyone involved hopes that they won't get caught and that they will get to Munich safely. From there they are then split up across the whole of the Federal Republic. I really could feel how nervous the people on our bus were. For me that was a very negative experience, and I have thanked God more than once that I am allowed to live in Germany. Some people, especially from Iran and Syria, somehow still manage to make it to our country. If they apply for asylum, the first thing our authorities check is whether they have already been registered in another EU country. If that's the case, then they have to go back to this country. Of course this presupposes that the country involved is politically and economically stable.

Ali entered the country from Sweden, which is a safe country today, as far as our politicians are concerned. It makes no difference that the people will very often be deported again, even though the conditions that await them in their country of origin will be intolerable and they could even end up in prison. Ali does not welcome that prospect, as this situation would mean his life was in danger. He has been commuting backwards and forwards between Magdeburg and Sweden ever since his application for asylum was rejected. Our town had to keep on taking him back until the next time he was due to be deported. But no decision will be possible in the future either, because our government cannot interfere in Sweden's internal politics. Ali has come to Magdeburg four times and would have kept on doing so, because he just can't go back to Pakistan. For me this has always been another unsatisfactory situation, because I noticed that I just couldn't do anything to help this young man. I kept on praying to God, asking him to save Ali from this suffering or from this fate, but it's not that easy. At the start of April 2015 I got a call from someone who worked on the psychiatric ward of one of the hospitals in Magdeburg. Ali had yet again tried to take his own life. He had told her that I was the only person in Magdeburg that had ever helped him or he could trust. Three weeks later he was suddenly standing in my office, after he had been discharged by the hospital. It was a Wednesday and of course Wednesday afternoon is when all of the doctors' surgeries are closed. Ali needed his medication urgently, but he didn't know where he was supposed to get this from. The hospital had discharged him without the tablets he had to take every day and which he would never get in any chemist without a prescription. I was at a loss as to what to do, but I trusted God and felt immediately that he had already worked out the solutions to these problems for me. The first thing I did was to call a colleague I fortunately knew personally from the Social Welfare Office. After a bit of back and forth, she said she was happy to issue a treatment note for the doctor, even though her office was also closed on Wednesdays of course. However, she also told me that the young man was now staying illegally in Germany, because the period in which his presence was tolerated had expired whilst he was in hospital. If the police caught up with him in this kind of situation, he would end up in prison. However the Foreigners' Registration Office was also closed, and I didn't want to send Ali there by himself anyway. So the first thing we did was to go to a lawyer, who was in his office, thank God. There was nobody in the waiting room at that time, which meant that he could talk to us straight away. There is no doubt in my mind that this was God in action. He told Ali that he had no chance. But after I had told him that he was in possession of a document from Sweden, which indicated that he was supposed to be deported to Pakistan, even though his life was in danger there, the situation looked a bit different. The lawyer did at least try to achieve the best possible outcome for the young man and has been representing him since then in matters involving officials who deal with foreigners. I always find the way God is in control of all these things astonishing. We then went to the Social Welfare Office, where the lady at reception was already waiting for us. The treatment note had already been prepared, which meant that we were able to save a lot of time. Finally I took Ali to the medical centre, where you can even get treatment in the afternoon, if you have an acute, medical problem. That day everything worked out so perfectly that I just couldn't stop being amazed.

Of course I knew that it was now very important for Ali to get in touch with other people. That's why I took him with me to church that Sunday. But he was extremely afraid that he would be punished by Allah for going there. That's why I couldn't get him to come with me back to the church again. But I think that eventually the time will be right for him to recognise God as well. At the end of May Ali came into my office and showed me his temporary resident's permit. In other words, his application for asylum is now also being assessed in Germany. And another few months later he got permission from the Foreigners' Registration Office to start training as a geriatric nurse. So he was one of the few people to be successful in this, even though he didn't have a full residence permit. But he has chosen to train in a job that is urgently needed in Germany. When he came back to my office one day, because he had to move out of the home where he had been staying, but only had a little bit of money available to pay his rent, I found a place for him in a flat that was shared by members of the Baptist Church. Who knows, perhaps that will even affect the rest of his life. God has once again saved a life, which is the most important thing.

Bashir, Safiola and Wahid play football

In the year after I became a Christian there's also this wonderful story about Bashir, Safiola and Wahid. Two of these boys come from Afghanistan and one of them is from Iran. They were sitting in our German class and one day they mentioned that they would love to play football in Magdeburg somewhere. Whilst there are a lot of football clubs in our city, the first problem is that it's virtually impossible to find a team for the over 18 age group and the second issue is that the boys were still living in a home for refugees at the time. I just couldn't really imagine that they would go to regular training sessions twice a week. However this is essential if you want to be an active member of a club. The trainers will not put up with irregular attendance and unexcused absences. So for me this issue was a non-starter, up until the day when a young Christian gave a presentation about his project for disadvantaged people during the service. He told us that he plays indoor football with young German kids once a week. That sounded ideal to me, as it would also give the boys I was looking after the opportunity to have some contact with young people from the area. So I talked to this trainer after the service and suggested that I could take my three lads to meet him the following week. He agreed to this and so that's what we did. On the day we had agreed we ended up standing outside the gym for a while ringing the doorbell. Eventually a young, bald man covered in tattoos opened the door for us. For a moment I was annoyed and this young man was also seemed a bit unsure. He undoubtedly thought that we had got the wrong address. From then on the boys in this really very diverse squad started training together. A few weeks later I wanted to get two more boys from Syria involved in this group and so took them to the training session. After the match the trainer came up to me and said that he couldn't let these two youngsters join, because otherwise the kids he was trying to reach out to would stop coming. I was so indignant and angry that the next day I sent him an e-mail telling him that what he had done was not right. He couldn't start by inviting new people and then withdraw the invite because they were foreigners. At the time, I actually thought that this was the real reason for his refusal to let them join. I also told him that I didn't think this was what Jesus would have done in this situation. His reaction was not very Christian. The young man wrote back to me, saying that his German boys spent most of their time on the streets and that some of them had even been to prison. It had taken months to build up trust with them and to get this football project started. Now he was just getting to the stage where they were starting to open up to him. They had accepted Bashir, Safiola and Wahid after some initial scepticism, beacause they were good football players. They had even got to the point where they wanted to lend them their football shirts for the next tournament, because the three boys I was looking after still didn't have any. I was totally amazed when I heard that. If I had known that these German kids were often violenc towards foreigners, I would never have taken my boys there. But that is exactly what God does. He brings people who would normally avoid each other together. At least the young German kids were starting to re-think their opinions about foreigners. They would never have laid a finger on their three new friends. I bet they would even have defended them in a sticky situation. That is remarkable by itself, but then God actually performed a miracle.

One day I got an e-mail from the trainer. He told me that he was still troubled by what had happened. He couldn't stop thinking about not letting the two Syrians join. So he wanted to get a new football project up and running and he needed my help. The plan was to book one of Magdeburg's numerous football pitches once a week. This is not normally possible, because the clubs guard their pitches like the Crown Jewels. They don't let anyone they don't know play on them and it always costs money. The young trainer had been very busy in the meantime and had found a few German football players who wanted to get involved in this project. Now all he needed was the immigrants as the final piece of the jigsaw. I told him that whilst I thought it was a very nice idea, the practicalities meant it was impossibe. Refugee families don't usually have any season tickets for public transport and so they can't travel right across town to get to a football pitch that's miles away. This is where God performed a real miracle. Bascially, just one club said it was happy to provide the pitch free of charge and it was only about ten minutes away from the home where the refugees were living. Anyone who says this was just a coincidence is really ignorant of all of the facts.

Denis can learn how to write

A few years ago I was dealing with a Jewish immigrant from Odessa, whose life up to that point had not been easy due to various issues in his family. He had had some problems whilst at school, which meant that he had never learnt to read, count or write. There is very little prospect of Denis starting a job, but the members of his family just didn't want to accept or admit this. There was hardly anyone who wanted to support this young man in finding a job or an apprenticeship, because difficulties kept on cropping up. The miracles happened at the end of 2011, so shortly after my conversion. Denis was supposed to start a vocational orientation programme in the craft trades the following summer, the aim of which was to help him find out which job was actually the best fit for him and whether he would be capable of completing vocational training. I had virtually given up on this case already, because his grandparents were not being co-operative and had categorically turned down any rehabilitation initiatives for their grandson, as their opinion was that Denis was completely normal. They always associated rehab with the idea of people with mental disabilities, which to be honest also included the young man, as far as I was concerned. They wanted him to start a completely normal apprenticeship in a trade in 2012. This did not fit in with the proposed placement he was offered by the Employment Agency based on his psychological report.

The situation was hopeless, but one day his grandparents quite unexpectedly declared that they were happy to have a look at the training centre for young people with special needs. They were delighted as soon as they realised that the young people seemed just as normal as their own grandson at first glance. I had been trying to persuade the family for months without any success and all of a sudden they changed their minds without much interference from me. What's more, as Denis had just had to come off another programme because it was too advanced for him, he was basically in limbo. I had been informed that there is an institution in Magdeburg that offers tutoring to pupils at affordable prices. I got a quote from the teacher and submitted it to the advisor who was dealing with Denis at the job centre. Incredibly, the young man was given a grant of 1,800 Euros to help him learn to read and write over the next six months. As I was talking to the woman who worked there, she told me that she had never had a case like this and she could not understand why such a large amount was approved. Help on a scale like this is often only guaranteed if a positive change or an advantage in terms of a job for the person being assisted can be identified. This was nowhere near the case with Denis. At the time noone dared predict what sort of job he might end up doing.

At the time I felt that God was very close. The young man was able to catch up on a few years of education, but to be honest I don't know if that was enough time to cover everything he had missed. This has not helped Denis start an apprenticeship yet, but the fact that he can at least read now is extremely useful. In the end, he managed to get himself a job as a building labourer in the summer of 2014. He would not have been able to find the right job offer on the Internet without these reading skills. However, the issues he has will always be a problem for him, because he can't remember instructions for very long. That is why the jobs he has had up to now with various employers have always been short term. In March 2015, the young man was again given the opportunity to be involved in a literacy programme lasting several years, after his new advisor at the job centre had stood up for him and found this being offered on the Internet. I don't know what this young man is doing today. I lost contact with him and his family, perhaps because he was finally able to move out and get away from the clutches of his grandparents. At that time I also talked to his grandmother about God and showed her that there are no coincidences with the Lord. She told me that she prays to God every day as a devout Jew and asks Him to help, because the members of her family are all ill and she wants her grandson to find a job eventually. Their rabbi had also come to their house and had prayed for her. But nothing had changed, which is why she sometimes doubted whether God actually helps anyone. I think that these believers have the wrong attitude about the Creator. Of course the Lord answers prayers, even if He doesn't always. But we cannot just assume that His decisions are always the right ones. So if someone is not healed, then it's horrible from our point of view. But as we don't know what His reasons are, we have to assume that there is a much better solution for this situation. Anyone who is a believer knows that life in the hereafter is much nicer than it is here on Earth. It is possible that God wants to shorten the lives of some people on Earth to end their suffering and to give them a much better life instead. This fact is definitely one hundred percent true in the case of my own parents. Both of my parents were terribly ill and were in severe pain before they died. But I am sure that they are fine now. A change of perspective would not have been a bad thing for Denis and his family, which is something I also told his grandmother. Instead of asking God every day to solve the problems the family was having, they should have been grateful for the good things in the future He had already done for them. Showing gratitude is always better than complaining and asking for things every day. She said that she would heed this advice. I felt a particular responsibility for this family for a long time. They are also some of God's chosen people. They might only seek out their rabbi whenever they need help from the worshippers there. He will not send them away, but these situations are definitely not pleasant for him. It states in the Bible that we should not just take, but we should also give to others. These people have still not understood that properly to this day. That is why they are never satisfied. They should be grateful that God has given them the opportunity to emigrate to Germany. Life in the Ukraine is so much harder nowadays. I hope that the whole family finds more balance and is not always trying to place the balme for their unfortunate situation on other people. It is unrealistic for Denis to pray for an apprenticeship, but I know that God is also at hand to protect this young man. I dare say that life would be better for Denis and his family if they welcomed God into their lives even more.

My unknown friend Paul

The following story started for me in October 2012, when an older woman, who was someone I only vaguely knew, told me about her grandson. Whilst the fate of this young man would have touched me a great deal in my former life, I would never have done anything to help someone I had not yet met personally. Paul's life story is so dramatic and awful that I feel so much pity for him to this day. I'm having a hard time not being angry with the people who are responsible for destroying his childhood. Paul is the son of a controlling and domineering father and a mother who is not at all assertive. The three of them lived together for the first two years of his life. Paul's father, who had been forced to experience violence and oppression from his father in his own childhood, started bullying his partner within a very short space of time and so she became incredibly scared of him. She still has this fear even today. He tortured her psychologically and used very hurtful and degrading language towards her. His parents separated when Paul was two years old. The court decided that his biological father should receive the right of access to his son. That meant that Paul later spent the weekend with him every two weeks. It didn't take long for his mother to realise that her son's behaviour was changing. Every time he came back home, he treated her with contempt and disdain, he posed naked in front of the mirror and grabbed men he didn't know by body parts that such a small child should not be familiar with. The Youth Welfare Office rejected his mother's application to stop his father having access. This led to the boy becoming more and more unbalanced. In the meantime his mother had a new partner and a little girl was now part of the family too. His mother was at a loss when it came to dealing with the boy's increasingly aggressive behaviour, his stepfather reacted by hitting him. Even back then Paul should have seen a psychologist, who would have perhaps found out the truth. But there was no indication that the Youth Welfare Office needed to do this, to use the proper bureaucratic language. When Paul also became violent towards his sister, his mother didn't want to have him in the house any more. She wanted him to go into a children's home or to a foster family. However the court decided that he should in future live with his father, who was the given sole custody of him. So Paul has been living with a man since April 2012, who intimidates and pressurises other adults, which is something he has also done frequenetly in the past. Nobody from the Youth Welfare Office dares say anything against him. Whilst I don't know him personally, I can quite imagine that he knows how to make other people panic.

Paul's nan told me that the boy was totally desperate at the start of October 2012 and asked her for help. He wanted to go back home to his mum and his sister. It seems unbelievable, but nobody reacted to this request, neither his own mother, nor the Youth Welfare Office or the Criminal Police. Over the next few days I wrote to every institution I could think of, as I tried to make the boy's messed-up life slightly more bearable at least. It is astonishing how much ignorance and indifference there is from every side even to this day. The family support worker, who up to then had never lifted a finger, felt personally attacked and the school followed his father's instructions that nobody was allowed to speak to Paul. I just cannot imagine how a child like this must feel, when they have been disappointed by every adult. The State Youth Welfare Office passed the case back to the Youth Welfare Office here, which never did anything. At least the member of staff involved led us to believe that there was probably no chance of success as long as the boy declined to say anything against his father in court. Eventually I sent a letter to the judge who was dealing with the case at the Family Court, in which I asked her to review the conditions that had been imposed on the father, when he was given sole custody of his son, who then went to live with him. My information was then passed on to the

Youth Welfare Office and the members of staff there gave Paul's father a copy of my letter. So much for data protection and me trying to do the right thing. Most people wouldn't even bother trying any more after something like that happens.

After the man had unsuccessfuly tried to threaten me when he rang me at work, I got a letter from his lawyer, demanding a payment of about 450 Euros for slander because of the accusation I had made against him. I then sent this blackmail letter to the court, which most likely then made it clear to the lawyer what it thinks of actions like this. Whilst the boy was later asked in court about the accusation of abuse that had been made against his father, he was obviously too scared to say anything against him and will not say anything in the future either. The only thing the State Criminal Office told me was that they could only get involved once a crime has been committed. I had found out from one of my friends that the court actually has the right to notify everyone involved in a legal dispute about my letter and so my information would be passed on. In the first few weeks I was actually worried that the father would try to get revenge on me, especially as he is very reluctant to accept defeat. And losing against a woman is something he just can't cope with. God intervened in these events, because it was a miracle that the father didn't take any further action against me and just gave up. Since then he has left Paul alone, which is not entirely a bad thing. His father is now worried about doing anything wrong and is being careful not to do anything illegal. I spoke to Paul's grandmother on 30.06.2014. She told me that her grandson was finally ready to get away from his father. I took that as my cue to get involved again, because it's important that the boy feels that he wants to change his own situation of his own accord. The Youth Welfare Office had got a new director a few months previously. And so on 01.07.2014 I sent another letter to the Youth Welfare Office, in which I once again made reference to the shortcomings of the people who worked there. After the Office decided that they didn't need to react to this letter, I approached one of the members of staff at the Town Council in the middle of July 2014. He forwarded the matter to the town councillor, who also did not show any reaction to my accusations about these shortcomings. The letter I sent to the councillor in person at the end of August 2014 also remained unanswered. It is shocking that the people who have these responsibilities didn't do anything to find out the truth. Paul needed help, because he has been living alone in the flat for months and was completely on his own. His father would leave him for weeks and was living with his new partner. As far as I'm concerned this is an unacceptable and intolerable situation, as an adolescent should not be forced to live in these circumstances. Even so, it's a miracle that Paul has survived the last few years almost without a scratch. In the summer of 2014 he got back in conctact with his nan and his mother. Since then they have been meeting regularly over increasingly long intervals. They now also spend Christmas and Easter together. God has been protecting this boy the whole time. For me, the fact that he had found some friends who have had a positive influence on him is one particular sign of this. These boys support each other, which meant that in the end he wasn't completely alone. He now has a girlfriend and is doing an apprenticeship. Contact with his father has stopped. His relationship with his sister, his mother and his nan is better again now as well. I'm sure he will occasionally regret the fact that it took him so long to get back in contact with the people who really love him. His nan told me that he is very unassuming. He is pleased about every new piece of clothing, every new pair of shoes and is always grateful. God has answered prayers for Paul from many Christians, by giving him an environment in which he was able to develop at a relatively steady pace.

However none of the relevant authorities should take any credit for this. What disturbs me most of all was that both the Family Court and also the Youth Welfare Office and the Family Support Worker never checked whether my accusations were justified or whether the conditions that were imposed on his father had been met. If they had kept their eye on Paul, then he would at least have got some psychological counselling, which was very important for him. But everyone involved left Paul to his own fate. I wonder whether they can still go to bed and sleep at night with a clear conscience, because they didn't do their job, which is protecting young people. God has often given bountiful blessings to people who have been mistreated by life. Paul can give a lot of help and support to other people who are in a similar situation to him and perhaps will even do that one day. I would like to use this story to show how people who have become Christians act and in particular what motivates them to do things. If I hadn't been one hundred percent sure that Jesus was protecting and supporting me all the time, I would have been much more afraid of revenge and would have stopped being involved in the story much earlier. However it is much more likely that I would never have offered my help, because the suffering of a stranger never affected me like that before. Because I'm aware that God will never abandon us if we live by his commandments and take action, I can also do things personally that might even be dangerous. Tht was the first time that somebody tried to accuse me of slander in court. But threats like this just bounce off me now, because I know that God loves justice and will always make sure that the truth is revealed in situations like this. The saying "pride comes before a fall" applies to anyone involved who has done something wrong. They will receive the judgement and punishment they deserve, because they left the boy in a life of misery due to their ignorance and indifference. But I'm not interested in making accusations against anyone. It's not my place to do that, because I am full of sin myself and in truth I have done enough things that were unjust in my own life. Even Paul's parents will have to take responsibility for their behaviour one day. It will not help them much if they point out that they had a troubled childhood themselves. It really is sad that certain ways of behaving seem to be inherited time and time again, but anyone above a certain age is responsible for their own actions. I hope that all of those officals who work for the authorities but did not live up to their responsibilities towards children and so failed in their duty, also recognise the truth so they can be saved. I hope that they then realise how much suffering they caused the people they were supposed to be protecting through their own failure to take action.

Biene's performance with the dance group

At the start of 2013 there was an event that affected my own family. Our daughter had been playing guitar at her music school for a few years, even though she never showed a great deal of interest or dedication. This changed abruptly when she and with three other boys were allowed to play together and rehearse for the "Young people playing music" competition. Suddenly she had a goal she was working towards, because playing in a group is always more enjoyable. The kids really got into it and rehearsed intensively for six months. I was really astonished by what they produced, because I hadn't expected that it would all sound so good. However, Biene also has a second hobby and it's something she has become passionate about. She has been going to a dance school since she was four and she has been dancing in "hip hop formations" since she was nine. This requires a lot of training, fitness and committment, even if it perhaps doesn't look like it to the uninitiated. The kids sometimes train three times a week before a competition. You need to be committed to this sport, or you won't practise as intensively as you need to. Biene's guitar teacher had told us when the rehearsals started that the music competition would take place in the middle of January 2013. That fitted into my daughter's plans very well, because a dance competition would be happening in the Netherlands on the last weekend in January. However, at the start of January, after I had asked him for the exact date again, he then told me that the music competition had been moved to the last weekend in January. I was totally schocked, because a situation had now arisen to which there was no solution. At the time I had often told my daughter that only a miracle can help in a situation like that. She should start praying for one, which of course is what I did too. God doesn't just send us solutions to our problems, even if we ask him to. We have to be proactive ourselves, if we want something to change. Initially I just waited, hoping that the situation would be resolved just with God's help and without me doing anything. However, after there was no prospect of a solution being found, I had to talk to the music teacher. Doing this was really not easy for me, because I knew that if the worst came to the worst, the others would take their frustration out on Biene. And that's also exactly what it seemed would happen at the time. When I told the teacher that Biene wouldn't be in Magdeburg on this weekend, the mother of one of the boys almost blew her top. After all, our kids had been rehearsing for months, and now it seemed it would all have been for nothing, because my daughter wouldn't be there. To make the situation clearer, I should explain that Biene couldn't miss either of the competitions. The guitar group could only perform if everyone was there. If one member of the group falls ill at short notice, then they all miss out. And with formation dancing, the dancers rely on each other anyway, especially as Biene frequently takes on the role of the lead dancer. However, the music teacher must have realised that it was mainly his mistake, because he hadn't told us about the date of the performance, even though he had known for months. And that was also the reason why he was now doing everything he could to find a solution.

In the end there is always a way of getting round the situation, especially if you ask God for help. Whilst the music school competition still took place on that specific weekend, some of the competitiors were able to postpone their performances until February, because they were having exactly the same sort of difficulties we were. That was certainly the case with some of them. Of course looking back, this was also a weight off Biene's shoulders, because she had felt very bad about it all. She basically didn't want to let anyone down, even if the boys were definitely not as important to her as her dance partners. I have reminded her about what happened with this quite a few times, whenever there has been a similar situation with apparently no solution. Unfortunately people tend to have short memories about this sort of thing. So I don't know how much the shock and the feeling of relief actually affected my daughter and whether she still remembers it today with the same intensity as she did at the time. In any case, the whole thing left a deep impression on me. I am convinced that there would not have been any solution to this problem unless God had got involved. Before then, the music competition had never been delayed for any of the competitors. Of course non-believers could now say that this is nothing special, but I know deep down inside me that God helped us out a great deal with this situation.

Fabi's new apprenticeship

I was also just as certain in March 2015 when our son Fabian had to apply for a place on an apprenticeship. He didn't want to go to university after he finished school. Instead he wanted to start an apprenticeship to become an industrial management assistant. I would never have believed that the application phase would be such a stressful time. If you want to work in a prestigious company, you have to pass several tests and persuade the human resources department that you are the right person for the job. A few years ago I went on a training course about "Young people applying for an apprenticeship". We were told how the entrance examinations are organised at "Euroglas", which was one of the major employers. At the time I was immediately impressed by this company, because I could feel that it had a healthy working environment and the whole company seemed to have a very good structure. I also told my son that I would be pleased if he got a training place at this company. He had to take several tests and have a number of interviews, during which he also found that the people who worked in the human resources department there were very friendly towards him. From the beginning Fabian felt very much at ease and that they were taking him seriously. In April 2015 he found out that he had got one of the four training places. God helped both me and my son in this situation too. It was absolutely not a coincidence that I had also had the opportunity to have a look at this company years before. He finished his training in the summer of 2018 and is now studying business information systems at university after all. I had been praying for both Sabrina and Fabian, although it's now obvious to me looking back that God has always made the very best decisions for our whole family and of course I'm very grateful to him for this. Both of our children went to the most highly-rated kindergarten in Magdeburg. I was listening to the radio in the car once when I heard that there had been an annual test comparing the various kindergartens in our town. The Protestant kindergarten in the district of Diesdorf kept on being put in first place in these tests. I was still pregnant at the time, but I decided that I wanted my first child to go to this kindergarten. As we don't live in that part of town, we probably wouldn't have got a space. The waiting list for interested parents is of course very long even today. Preference is given to children who live locally. The parents put up with their children getting a Christian education, even if they are non-believers themselves. But children from a Protestant denomination also have a chance. We eventually did get a place and were incredibly happy about this. Of course four years later it was then very easy for our youngest to be accepted into this kindergarten as a sibling. I think it's really wonderful they were both being taught about the Gospel, even if they have drifted away from the truth a bit over the years. Deep down they know that they got a very good education when they were young children and were very well looked after in their childhood.

Afterwards, both children were then able to go to the primary school in the district of Diesdorf, even though we didn't live in its rural and still very friendly catchment area. This was ony possible because I submitted an application to the education authority personally. I wanted my children to grow up in an environment where they would be well looked after. Sabrina would not automatically have been given permission to go to this primary school, because her older brother was already going to the grammar school by then. Even the headteacher of the primary school was surprised about the education authority's decision at the time. But I'm most grateful for the fact that our daughter was able to go to the "Oskar Kämmer School" from year 5. She was one of the lucky ones to be selected from 150 applicants. However, they could only accept 24 children. This school, which is partly privately financed, teaches pupils up to year 10. But the general atmosphere is quite a bit better than in a state school, because it's smaller and the teachers can give the pupils more individual care thanks to the financial resources they have available to them. Sabrina's best friend, whom she had known since they were at kindergarten, also got one of these oversubscribed places. My daughter decided that she wanted to become a primary school teacher whilst she was still at school. That's why she started going to a specialist college in the summer of 2017, so she could get her vocational diploma after two years. Normally you can only train to be a primary school teacher at university. But the laws about this have been

47

changed as there is an urgent need for primary school teachers. Now the universities also accept applicants who are only entitled to study at a polytechnic. I think that it is the right career for her, because she was full of enthusiasm every day when came home from her work placement in her first year at the specialist college. As I said before, both my academic career and those of my children have been steered towards the right paths by God. This is one thing I thank him for every day, because it's not something that should be taken for granted.

I pray a lot for my family, my friends, acquaintances and clients. But if several people pray for the very same thing, this obviously has a big effect. Unfortunately this definitely does not often happen with me personally, which means that often it's just me asking God for certain things. When I moved to Magdeburg in 1995 to be with my partner, I was already aware that I would be the only Christian for miles around, because everyone I know and all of my friends and relatives are non-believers. This situation has still not changed even today. But of course I have not avoided them, even since I found God. Instead I have always told them about the new things I have realised, but without pushing this too much. Forty years of Socialist education have left their mark. In Magdeburg there are only a very few Catholics and Protestants who believe in God. However, these have been joined by Orthodox Christians and Jewish people since the collapse of the Soviet Union and the arrival of refugees from Eritrea. The same applies to the Christians who already became believers when they were in Iran or Pakistan and have had to leave their country because of this. So here we have a lot of things going on with Christians who have just received their calling and want to prove themselves and others who want to become a follower of Jesus. As a result of this unique situation, refugees from countries where Islam is the state religion also find their way to Christ, because people they have met have told them about their faith and then take them along to a service. Most of these people come from Afghanistan and so the main thing they like about becoming a Christian is that this is a peaceful religion and is not just based on restrictions and rules. They get a sense of the inner peace emanating from many members of the congregation. However most of the Christian congregations in Magdeburg are led by liberal pastors, so you can perhaps imagine how sad the situation seems in this large town. But I keep thinking to myself that God will certainly have had his reasons for sending me to this area in particular. His intention is probably for me to influence my unchristian surroundings, so that Magdeburg can be really inundated with people who have woken up in the near future. At least my partner's family is so tolerant that they allow me to live my life according to my faith. They also agreed to our children being baptised. However, their distancing themselves from God more and more due to the influence of their enviroment was predictable, even though both of them went to a Protestant kindergarten and so have been given the basic essentials. But at school most of the ideas they are taught are unchristian and some theories that have long since been disproved are accepted as facts. Take the theory of evolution for example. As a mother, I'm then left with the choice of deciding whether my children should just go with the flow, so that they don't become outsiders, or whether we make a stand against this idea that is accepted above all others. The latter takes a lot of courage and endurance, that I was unfortunately unable to muster and so I never asked my children to do this either. I still pray every day, both for my family as well as for my friends, as I still want them to recognise the truth, because I definitely don't want them to be unable to find their way back to God.

A few years ago, I was working with a colleague who was pregnant at the time this story happened. On one occasion I asked her in passing how she was feeling. You don't normally expect an answer to this sort of question, and you certainly don't expect anything negative. The woman should have been delighted, because she would be having her baby soon, but she wasn't happy. She told me that things weren't going well for her, but I didn't respond to what she said. I thought that this was just her mood swings coming out. A few weeks later, after her son had been born, this woman threw herself off of the roof of an eleven-storey block of flats, because her marriage had broken down. She had apparently tried to save the marriage by having a baby, but even this little boy did nothing to change the situation. Since then I have often wondered whether I could have perhaps helped this woman, just by listening to her that one time. Whilst that is very unlikely, we don't know everything after all. One word can sometimes change someone's whole life, one wrong word can also do the same. That's why we can't just keep using meaningless phrases, instead we should consider what we're saying very carefully. We ask these rhetorical questions just to be polite and because they've become fashionable, we don't expect an honest answer anyway. Because who really wants to know how someone else is feeling nowadays? If that person then gives an honest answer and mentions that they have got problems, most people just aren't prepared for this at all and don't want to listen. But it's very important that we do, especially in moments like that. We have to pay more attention to our fellow human beings. People are suffering from loneliness more and more even in big cities, because everyone is just thinking about themselves. But God actually created us to be happy when we're living in a community. Ignorance and indifference are the biggest problems of our time. That is why lonely people often look for a refuge in sects and in dubious groups. Of course they are often welcomed with open arms in these and might even feel happy, because it gives them a wonderful feeling of belonging, which they miss so much in their daily life. This is the ideal environment for Satan to flourish, because places like this, which mainly involve worshipping some self-proclaimed prophet and healer, are where there is nothing to stop him exerting a bad influence on the people concerned.

In contrast, if they have a good grounding in a congregation and they take their faith really seriously, converted Christians do good deeds. We should show love when we meet people and help them whenever we can. These actions always bear fruit, even if it's not immediately obvious most of the time. Sometimes the positive results of our efforts may only be recognised decades later. Robert once told me that when he was working with his friends as a missionary in Halle, they often came into contact with people who were addicted to drugs and alcohol. They showed the people who had succumbed to addiction what spending time together in peace can look like. One of them stopped drinking many years later. A lot of people thought that this would never happen, but we should never give up hope, especially with things like this. We should always put our trust in God, because only He knows when the right moment to be converted is for every individual. Then He also speaks to them personally, whether it's through words, through pieces of writing in a book or even through a video like in my case. One very special type of fruit is love, because it really can change people. Even a friendly word to someone we don't know at all shows that person that we care about them. It's the little things in life that make our fellow human beings feel grateful. And we should always bear in mind that in the right circumstances what starts as a small shoot can grow into a big tree. A friendly hello to someone first thing in the morning today can cause someone to start following Jesus tomorrow. People remember anyone who has given them encouragement and supported them when they were in need, even if it's just with some sympathetic words.

Our lives should be based on loving each other. This is God's wish. God will reward anyone who lives according to this principle and trusts others unselfishly, who passes on love and provides support. However if our actions are just calculated to look good, then whilst they will help other people, they will not benefit us in any way. This is one thing that I personally find is a big struggle. We have to consider very carefully which words we choose, because God will never forget them and they will be important to Him when He passes judgement. I often find myself moaning about other people, if they are talking what I think is rubbish, doing stupid things, treating others badly or thinking that they are better than anyone else. Then I soon start wanting to swear, which is really not very Christian. I also talk about other people behind their backs. Or I criticise people, because I think they are living their lives the wrong way or they are doing things that are unjust or are just not doing things in the right way in my mind. That is also arrogant of me, because what gives me the right to judge other people? I know that this is one of my biggest faults and one of my most ingrained habits. But of course I am trying to choose my words more carefully. An intelligent person thinks before speaking. I can't always say that about myself, because my reactions are often too impulsive. Every person is responsible for their own life in a different way, because we are all very different. If I just think about my situation, then I think that this is quite a challenge for me. I have also been given a great deal of freedom by the Lord to be able to live up to this responsibility.

However, despite God giving us this freedom, we are all responsible for our own actions at all times. Even if Satan leads us astray with poor circumstances in our lives, the wrong sort of friends, drugs or anything similar, we cannot buy our way out of this obligation. I think that I can serve God best by bringing children and young people of various nationalities closer to the Gospel. It does not matter to God at all how respected we are in society and also what job we do as a result of this, because we can only earn what we truly deserve through him anyway. This thought reassures me a lot, because it means I have become more at ease with people working in more senior positions. If I know that these people have only got his job through the grace of God, then I don't need to be scared of them any more. I treat these people with respect, but not with unconditional obedience and subservience. And if I notice that a person I am working with directly is behaving dishonestly and abusing the responsibility they have been entrusted with for their own purposes, then this respect will vanish completely. I am fairly sure that these people soon realise that they're dealing with someone who will not tolerate dishonesty and wrongdoing. In these moments the Holy Spirit is also exerting an influence on them, which I can recognise in most cases from their facial expressions and their gestures, but especially from the lack of confidence in their demeanour. I then think that it's fortunate that everyone is equal before God. Even influential personalities cannot have unrestricted power and impose the laws and rules they have made themselves on everyone. The Lord can see every injustice and will also hold these people to account one day, regardless of whether they are now working as a judge, a lawyer, a public official, a director of social institutions, a politician or an official at a public authority or agency. But in those specific cases where I have had to deal with dishonest, ignorant, power-hungry people with no respect for others and no conscience, I hope that their misconduct is uncovered while they are still alive, so that not too many people are affected and have to suffer and that they can also still be saved themselves.

God particularly loves choosing people to perform great services and tasks, who strictly speaking are not at all suited to these jobs, because they are too shy, not articulate, not intelligent enough or are even just not particularly outgoing. If I'm honest, I also belong to this group of people. I can still remember very well how few friends I had at school when I was younger and that I was an outsider because of my shy personality. I used to find socialising with other people incredibly hard. That is why I was often alone back then, which was something I didn't like that much personally. If I look at myself today, then I often really do wonder where I got all of the energy to do what I'm doing. And then it becomes clear to me again and again that I would be able to achieve absolutely nothing at all without the Holy Spirit. From this we can draw the conclusion that the Lord has no favourites and nobody is of greater importance to Him. If anything, He wants everyone to be saved by recognising the truth. God will not let anyone be sent to eternal damnation deliberately, by denying them salvation. The Lord will not condemn anyone to an endless existence in Hell or preordain this fate for anyone, because we are able to decide ourselves how our fate will turn out. We bear the sole responsibility over whether we receive eternal life or not. God will not send anyone to their doom, because he loves every human being. He knew that stubborn people would never find their way to Him, even before the creation of the world. Before we can say yes to God, He has already made His decision long before and chosen us. We should be really happy about this. But He also respects our free choice and waits patiently for us to decide to spend our lives with him. We would not be accepted by Him without His mercy. God alone has known from the start which people have been chosen by Him and who will one day decide to follow Him of their own free will. But as we can be certain that God will accept every prayer asking for conversion, we should make our own request to convert to Jesus. When we pray to receive God's forgiveness, we are only completing what God decided for us thousands of years ago. That is why I would suggest to everyone that it's better to accept the sacrifice Jesus made today instead of waiting until tomorrow, because our time is limited. On the other hand, God has infinite patience. At any moment He is waiting for more and more people to recognise His loving nature and accept the mercy of His salvation.

The Safi family comes to Germany

Mr. Safi, an elderly man from Afghanistan, came to see me in my office at the start of 2012. He told me his story, which is one I still don't really understand even today. But I think it's important to tell you about it. Mr. Safi used to work as a teacher. He lost his right hand and half of his left leg in a rocket attack whilst he was at a bus stop waiting for the next bus. Later on he worked as the manager of a children's home for the German organisation "Children need us" in Kabul. This association was financed entirely from donations and had set itself the task of taking sick children from Afghanistan to Germany, so they could have the surgery they needed here. At the same time a home was set up in Kabul for destitute orphans and children whose parents were unable to look after them. It was a good place, because they got an education and several meals a day there. The director of the association was even given a Bambi award for his dedication. I think that this commitment is really very impressive, but in retrospect, it turned out there was a lot more behind all this. Mr. Safi told me that 21 of the children who had come to our country for an operation had never gone back home again. As a result, he and his family were threatened by the parents of these children, because they thought that it was his fault. Mr Safi sent a lot of e-mails to the director of the charity in Germany to find out where these children were. Every time he got the same answer back from him, which said that they had to stay here even longer for the purpose of rehabilitation. By this time some of the children had already been in our country for more than six years. At the start of 2012 Mr. Safi travelled to Germany himself for a meeting with the director of the association, because he wanted to see for himself what was going on in the place where it was happening and find a solution to the problem. He was bitterly disappointed, because absolutely no one here wanted to help him take the children back to their parents in Afghanistan. I couldn't believe it when he showed me the photos of the little ones, some of whom were still babies, and the stories behind them. We live in a country where the legal system is still working. There had to be some way of shedding some light on the situation. However, after a meeting with his lawyer, it was clear to me that some things should be kept quiet here. Mr. Safi's family had to go into hiding in Afghanistan as soon as he left his home country, because otherwise they would have been killed by the disappointed parents. His children were not able to go to school for months and his wife was not allowed to leave the house where they had found refuge for very long. It's a miracle that they are all still alive today. I told this story to various newspaper publishers and TV stations, because I knew that the only way to bring about any change in this situation was to publicise the story. At the same time I wrote to the courts and ministries that could be able to come up with a solution to this problem. The reaction of the Foreign Office in Berlin was the one I found the most interesting. I was told that they knew about the story there, because death threats had already been made against employees of the German Embassy in Kabul precisely because of this. However, they can't do anything themselves, because it's a matter that should be sorted out in Afghanistan. The Ministry of the Interior in Berlin was also of the same opinion. However, the state prosecutor's office in Duisburg even said that there was not enough evidence to justify a ban when we asked to them to take a closer look at this organisation and issue a court order banning it. This was a case that needed to be sorted out in Afghanistan. However,

I did not share this opinion, as this association was registered here in our country and was being financed by donations from Germany. Initially, the media seemed to be very interested in this case, but then all suddenly backed off, because the people who worked for the press and the TV had been told not to report about this by their superiors. Nothing was done, even though the state prosecutor's office in Duisburg had collected a large number of dossiers about these unsolved cases. One day, after I had already given up hope of any sort of change, "Report Munich" showed a very interesting documentary. It had actually found someone to look into this story more closely. This report included interviews with the authorities in

Germany, although they all came up with excuses. But some reporters did actually go to Afghanistan themselves, to question people in the area. The information they found out there was that several families were actually waiting for their children to come back and they are still waiting today. However there were also some criminal things that came to light. The families were led to believe that the director of "Childreen need us" was a doctor. After he had won their trust, he got the parents of the sick children to sign a piece of paper. They definitely thought it was a consent form for the children to be transported to Germany and for the surgery the children were supposed to be getting in our country. In fact they were signing an adoption certificate. Once the children were better, they were put up for adoption to German parents here in Germany. This was confirmed by several people in this report. For me this is pure human trafficking, which must be stopped immediately. Once these children had been staying here for several years and had also found a family to adopt them, the relevant Youth Welfare Offices decided that repatriating them to Afghanistan would be impossible. The welfare of the children would be put at risk, because life for them would be much tougher than in Germany. This attitude has not changed one bit to this day. Once these children reach adulthood, they can decide for themselves whether they want to stay in Germany. By then there would be no chance of this happening anyway, because they won't want to go back to their parents or to a country they don't know any more. Some of the children were only a few months old when they arrived in Germany. They probably have no idea where they really come from. However, nothing has ever been done for the children and their families in Afghanistan, even after this documentary was shown, which is why I am convinced that our government has simply closed the file on this issue. However, our state has agreed a compromise. Mr. Safi's family was granted asylum in Germany and is now also in Magdeburg.

I am fairly sure that their silence was bought, because Mr. Safi now makes strenuous efforts to avoid me. He is probably scared that I will ask him what happened. But I will not do that, because the case is closed as far as I'm concerned. Even I know when it's no longer worth fighting against injustice, because even the people who make the laws in this country are not honest and are very successful at stopping cases like this being resolved. But when I first started trying to find out what was going on, I really did pray frequently for the problem to be sorted out. The Holy Spirit gave me courage and perseverance. At the time, a lot of people were telling me to keep out of political issues like this, because it could get dangerous for me and for my family. I am still being told this today. Mr. Safi is someone who is well-known in Afghanistan, he was even in contact with the president of the government at the time. Today I think that there was no other solution to this delicate situation. Of course there were a lot of other people who got involved and tried to help this man from Afghanistan. God has restored justice for his family, with the pressure increasing, the "Children need us" association was finally banned too. Unfortunately the children's home had to close after Mr. Safi left the country, because it was impossible to find some suitable to take over. As far as the situation with the children themselves and their families in Afghanistan is concerned, it's not something I'm willing or able to pass judgement on. Perhaps staying here in Germany is actually the best solution for some of them. Their lives would be less comfortable there, to put it in the simplest terms. As far as the Safis and the head of that family are concerned, the reactions I have personally enocuntered have been completely different. Whilst some of his children definitely blame Germany for causing their personal misfortune, the others are just grateful that they have finally found a place of refuge after months of uncertainty. For me, Mr. Safi is the most puzzling, because he has rarely been honest towards me. On the one hand he is very grateful to me and has even said before that he would not have managed to bring his family to Germany without my help. On the other hand, he made a false statement about me to the police, because he thought it would help him. It would be normal for me to condemn this man for what he has done. And that's what I would have done once too. But now I just feel sorry for him and I ignore him.

In my view, one of the reasons the Islamic religion is absolutely unacceptable is because, as far as some Muslims are concerned, there is no problem with telling lies about people they think are non-believers, if it helps them. After I had told Mr. Safi that I am a devout Christian, he was so complimentary about Christianity and about Jesus. But his words have been forgotten now that his family is here. Today I think that in all of the months of the most intense discussions we had, he only ever told me things he hoped would give him an advantage. Mr. Safi is perhaps a very good example who illustrates how some followers of the Islamic faith behave in times of crisis. However Muslims and everyone else also believe in a Creator who made the Universe. They recognise the fact that God must exist, not least because of all of the living beings and all of the things that He created. But there is also the fact that every human being has had a conscience since the fall of mankind, which God also uses in many situations to show us on an emotional level when we consciously do something wrong. For most people, wrongdoing triggers negative emotions. God uses our conscience to remind us that we are disconnected from Him. Every human being on this earth is trying to find a connection to the Lord. We all carry this longing for Him in our hearts, because God gave it to us. But He also gave us the ability to think and exercise free will, so that we can decide how to live our lives ourselves. Because people have wanted to restore their relationship with God on their own terms, they have invented various divine beings or religions since the fall. They thought that they could find the way to God just by using made-up rules and rites and praying to apparently sacred objects. All of these human endeavours, which eventually turn out to be unsuccessful, are referred to as religion. I reject every religion without exception, because they are all based on rituals, objects and holy people that believers are expected to worship, but which were all invented by people. This also applies to the Christian church. I proclaim the Gospel alone and only base my actions on what is written in the Holy Scripture. Unless God has asked us to do certain things for Him in the Bible, then it is just a human concept. As far as I'm concerned, this includes worshipping saints in the Orthodox Church as much as venerating the "Holy Father" and the "Mother of God".

In reality, Martin Luther was not a perfect human being. Quite the opposite. In my view the position he adopted against Jewish people, especially at the end of his life, is nothing less than incomprehensible. How could he hate the People of God so much, even though he of all people must have known that Jesus died on the Cross for us all? He should have been glad about this, because he was also saved by this. The Jews were also persuaded by the Pharisees to have Jesus crucified. So it's the religious leaders themselves who should be judged more than anyone else. And God knows that even Luther was not without sin. His behaviour at the time would probably have been no different to what the Jews did in Jerusalem. They had been misled and thought that the Messiah would free them from Roman rule. When this didn't happen, their belief was that Jesus could not be the Messiah. Most Jews still believe this today. I can quite understand this way of thinking. However it is also possible - and this is backed up by written evidence - that Luther was particularly critical of the negative behaviour of some Jewish bankers. There are black sheep in every religious community. But we also have Luther to thank for the fact that the Protestant Church has found its way back as much as is possible to where the first Christians had once started, moving away from rituals and towards the Gospel. The earliest Christian congregations, which had emerged from the Jewish faith, only lived according to the teachings in the Gospel and so for me they are the only true Christian congregations to this day.

From San Francisco to Tel Aviv

In May 2013 I got a friend request on Facebook from a woman who now lives in Tel Aviv. This is not unusual, because this often happens with the statuses about the Gospel I post on there almost every day. People subscribe to my page, because they are hungry to find out more about God. Nothing more would have happened, if I hadn't realised that Mary comes from San Francisco when I looked at her profile. I have always found the USA interesting and so I asked her why she had moved to Israel from the USA, more out of curiosity than anything. That was the start of a long story, which did not turn out anything like what I had ever planned. But this is also a case where you can see how God gets involved, whenever He notices that we need His help. At the start we only exchanged messages about what our lives were like and how we mainly spend our time. It turned out that Mary had been bringing up three hormonal teenagers as a single parent for years. I don't mean that in a negative way, but anyone who has had to look after girls aged between 16 and 19 in their household will know what I'm talking about. I'm sure she always had enough to do and was fully occupied with her role of being a mother. But now it's just getting to the time where the chicks will soon be leaving the nest and are starting to spread their wings. They no longer need our help as often and are increasingly doing their own thing. For Mary, this means that she is now doing more with her own friends and without her children. They meet up quite often, but as a general rule, nobody is really interested in anyone else's problems. But Mary doesn't like to open up anyway and doesn't particularly like telling other people about her doubts, worries and needs. She is a very emotional person and so she sometimes struggles with mood swings. She was in a depressive phase just as we were getting to know each other, because the man she was in love with had left her. After chatting to her for hours, I was able to convince her that life can still be wonderful and worth living, even after a fiasco like that. Her fellow human beings often use her, because she is friendly with everyone but she is also too trusting. Whenever she was rejected by somebody she had put her trust in, she projected the blame for this onto herself. As she grew up without a father and her mother did not show her much love or pay her much attention when she was a child, she does not know what it feels like to be looked after and loved by your parents. The affection she gets from her children is of course another type of love.

And the very moment we got in contact with each other was when she had reached a low point. From the start I had the feeling that she needed some support deep within me and that God chose me for this task. He knows better than anyone which people meet each other's needs. Her situation was particularly bad at the time of the war in Gaza in the summer of 2014. Mary kept on losing more and more weight because of the stress and was actually as thin as a rake. But she has had a friend for three years who gives her and her family financial support. She works in his restaurant. In my view this is the best solution for her. At the end of October 2014 I spent ten days in Israel. I was travelling with a group from Franconia, to visit the original locations of some of the events mentioned in the Bible. Mary visited us in Jerusalem on the second day and spent the day with the group. We went sightseeing around the city and even went to a service that was held in German. For Mary this was a new experience, because she is Jewish. But she enjoyed it and we enjoyed each other's company a lot. Since then she has become even more important to me. This is probably due to the fact that I am well aware that the family is sitting on quite a powder keg in Israel. Clashes between Muslims and Jews can happen at any time in this small country, because no Muslim will ever recognise Israel as an independent state. But it's also because of the the fact that I admire this small person, because up to now she has dealt with her tough life as a single parent so well. Mary told me when we were in Israel that she would like to get to know Jesus. I gave her a Bible, but at the same time I also gave her a piece of advice, which was not to read the whole book in one go. For someone who has never had anything to do with the Holy Scriptures, that would definitely be too much. Another reason she didn't look at it was because she just wasn't ready to do that yet. I was baptised for the second time in my life on 30.10.2014, but this time it was in Jordan at the place where Jesus is believed to have been baptised. This baptism was the real reason for my trip to Israel. I wanted to show as an adult that I am a follower of Jesus. As a child you don't have any choice and most teenagers don't take being confirmed as seriously as they should when they're 14 either. I gave my testimony on the evening before I was baptised, when I told everyone about my conversion. My witness could also become a seed like this, which could be sown and then grow into a great oak. Even before the big event, God had basically shown me that He supported my decision. The baptism was performed by one of the pastors from the Protestant church in my State. I was told that they are not allowed to baptise a person a second time, because it is a sacrament. But neither he nor the pastor from my parish had any objections, because it was God's will. Today I believe that the Lord wanted to use this to show that even the State churches can become more open. There were three pastors in our group on this trip and I had some very lengthy discussions with them. My hope in doing this was that it would get one or other of them thinking so it would inspire them in their work. They have to tell their congregation that turning to God is the most important thing in a person's life. And they should ask people to talk about wonderful or amazing things they have experienced with God during the service much more often. When I told my fellow travellers the story of my own conversion just before I was actually baptised, some of them were so overwhelmed that they even started crying. The following morning the sky was very cloudy. It looked like it might start raining at any moment. But the exact moment I was being baptised was when the clouds parted and the sun shone through. Perhaps God also wanted to give a sign to show that we should just have faith that every human being can have a living relationship with Jesus whilst still here on Earth. I found this baptism very moving and will not forget it as long as I live. Today it is clear to me why it had to be a pastor who works for the Protestant Church in my state who baptised me. The Lord used this to show us that which Christian confession we belong to is totally unimportant to Him. The important thing is having faith in Him and the salvation we have been promised when Jesus gave his life for us. Anyone who confesses to Him will be saved. The policies of your church are not a factor any more.

In the ten days of our visit to Israel, we also visited historically important places in West Jordan. But even at that time you could feel that there was something in the air. In Bethlehem we even went to visit a Baptist congregation. Most of us have no idea just how much courage it takes to stay loyal to Jesus in an area like this where the potential for violence is so great. In Hebron we went to a small synagogue in the middle of the residential area. You would never realise that either of the two buildings are places of worship from the outside. Even so, I thought that these places more important than the large number of churches that were built by the Franciscans and the Orthodox Christians as they competed against each other. It's hard to imagine where Jesus gave his Sermon on the Mount, because there is a large church on this hill today. Access to the Temple Mount was blocked for the first time since 1967 the day after our visit there. Some members of our group had even seen the rabbi who was shot at and almost killed that day by an Arab Palestinian when we were on the Temple Mount. It was very disconcerting that the Muslims there were shouting "Allah is greater".

However the real miracle that God made happen for Mary did not happen until March 2015. Even at the start of the year I noticed that she was getting very desperate, because her situation seemed hopeless. Mary had been on a vocational training course for several years and would soon be taking her exam. Her laptop went missing when she moved into her new flat. She had saved all of the graphics files she needed for her final assessment on this. At the time she did not have enough money to by a new device. I sent her some. She invested it in a new laptop and was then able to reinstall the computer programme. That took a great deal of time and effort, but right from the start she was focussed on the aim of getting a job in this area once she had finished her training so that she could earn enough for herself and her family. Mary had reached her personal lowpoint in February 2015, because she realised that she often didn't understand what she had learnt and could not apply it. She was getting really desperate. But once again the advice I gave her was to put her trust in God and ask Jesus for help. In the weeks that followed she felt empowered and felt the strength returning to her own body. She arranged a few lessons with a tutor and, like a miracle, she was then able to understand the programmes. At the end of February she suddenly became terribly ill. Mary suffered from a cough for weeks, which could not be relieved with any antibiotics. This situation really was very disconcerting. No medication did anything. I really was getting very desperate and asked God for help every day. Eventually the doctor had to prescribe her cortisone. Mary had an appointment for an x-ray, which she did not go to straight away, because she was worried what the diagnosis would be. The suspicion was that she must have had pneumonia or perhaps something even worse. In the end she talked herself into it and it was a total surprise when the doctor told her the x-ray did not show anything. He couldn't explain this, because there had to be a reason for the persistent cough. I knew that my friend had this appointment. When I didn't hear anything from her for the whole day, I was already fearing the worst. So I rang her in the evening. Mary was completely overwhelmed by the fact that someone was worried about her. She even started crying whilst we were talking on the phone, because her own family hadn't even called her. I was very moved, although I had a few problems when she told me that. But it is also really hard to understand how someone must feel when they grew up without being protected as a child and so doesn't know the feeling of being loved. But God loves her just as she is. This was something she had never realised before. Up until the day I told her this, Mary could not accept herself, because she did not think she was worthy of being loved. She blamed herself for the fact that some people had turned their backs on her.

On 08.03.2015 I was praying for Mary's health to improve together with Robert, who had given his first sermon in a small congregation earlier that day. The miracle happened, because she trusted the healing power of Jesus unconditionally. After I told her about my joining Robert in prayer, she immediately stopped taking the medication that was poisoning her body. The way she saw it, this was the only way she would be saved, as nothing else had helped. I think this is one hundred percent faith and complete devotion to God. Mary's health was completely restored. However, the best thing about all of this is that she realised that Jesus is her saviour. He was the only one who could heal her. She had an exam she was really worried about on 11.03.2015. I told her that she just had to trust Jesus. He would be at her side and give her the strength and power she needs. Afterwards she told me that she had prayed to Jesus just before the exam. She knew everything and could even feel how she was being supported through the test. Sometimes God uses a really hopeless and desperate situation, which can be turned into something good. Mary now believes in the sacrifice Jesus made and so she has been saved. This was the best thing that could have happened to her. There are people who belive in the existence of God, but not in the Messiah. Whilst this is definitely a step in the right direction, it does not bring them salvation from death. Mary had also been a person of faith for the whole of her life. But she had not had any direct contact with God, because on Earth this can only happen through the Holy Spirit. Jesus is alive and He works in us. Through Him we receive the love, strength and knowledge we need, so we can be successful. In May 2015 I visited Mary in Tel Aviv. I had to learn that not all women are emancipated. The key to independence is education, without which it's impossible to practise a career of course, so you can stand on your own two feet financially. However, Mary has been dependent on other people for her whole life, especially in terms of money, and still is today. I got the impression that she copes with this situation really well. Perhaps relationships also work very well sometimes, because one partner sets the pace and the other one follows their instructions. If both of them are happy with this, you just can't say anything against it. I got to know her partner, but we didn't become friends, because he could not accept my independence. I've got a mind of my own and I don't need anyone to make decisions for me. But that is all this man knows and he is used to other people abiding by his instructions and wishes. At the end of 2016 I met up with my friend and her children again in Berlin, because that was when they came to Germany for a short trip. We spent a few hours together and we had a look around the capital. In 2015 I also visited a Messianic Jewish congregation during my trip to Tel Aviv, which mainly consists of Jewish immigrants from Russia and the Ukraine. I found the service very enjoyable, because I had the feeling that the people took their faith in Jesus seriously. Perhaps one day Mary will seek out this community and find some honest and sincere friends there. They can help her stay strong in her faith. She now knows that God can perform miracles. If I had not helped her, then the Lord would have sent someone else. God knows that Mary loves Him dearly, and so He looked after her. I am not the saviour of her life, even if it looks that way to her.

Ines, a role model for other people

I have known Ines ever since we studied at the College of Education in Magdeburg together. We were not best friends to begin with, because our characters are completely different. I am fairly sure that we would never have got to know each other better either, if God had not come into our lives. I really do believe that He made our paths cross, because it's most likely that I would not have gone looking for her on my own. We first got to know each other better when we worked together as leaders at a children's holiday camp. After that I sort of looked up to Ines as a role model, because at the time I was still very reserved and was not very confident in myself at all. In contrast, Ines seemed to have a fascinating effect on everyone. She was attractive, intelligent, determined and forward-thinking. At the time I even had something of an inferiority complex, because my results were not as good as those of my classmates. So I was pleased that we did some things together. Some students in our seminar group disapproved of this friendship and even openly showed their displeasure. Ines had a very dominant personality back then, and I almost always put my own wishes and desires second to hers. One of her most unpleasant characteristics was that she tended to judge other people purely on the basis of their personality or appearance, even if she was not exactly perfect herself. Of course I did not like that, but I tolerated this behaviour, probably because I would have loved to have been admired as much as her. People with leadership qualities always have an easier life and are never outsiders. They decide who belongs to their circle of friends. At the time I also went with the easy option all the time, because my self-esteem was at rock bottom. Ines and I did even chat about faith in God back then. I had never made a secret of the fact that I was a Christian, even if it was not that easy in the Socialist era. One day Ines told me that she was also a Protestant. I was probably the only person she had told this piece of information. As far as politics was concerned, she was like many others, as she was someone who just went with the flow, not wanting to have any problems or stand out from anyone else. Ines would have never made her faith in God public, especially as it was not that strong at the time anyway.

At one point she told me that she had always felt the urge to support people who were weak and outsiders like me. Perhaps that's what she thought was the motivation behind our friendship. This statement is not true however, because I also had other friends during my time as a student. But she must have found something interesting about me as a person, otherwise we would not have stayed friends for so many years. Ines had big plans for her future. She could only imagine spending her life with a doctor, lawyer or some other academic. But Ines was also gifted herself and a very good teacher, who was a dedicated professional. We lost contact with each other for a short time after we left college and we went our separate ways. I found out that she had moved to Bavaria and started a family there. We wrote letters to each other again at the start of the 1990s. She told me that she was an active member of a Protestant church and had been working at various schools as a German teacher. That was not as obvious as it sounds, because our diplomas are still not recognised in Bavaria today, even though we went through the same training as any other student teacher in Bavaria. Despite this, Ines was allowed to work at the University of Bayreuth and in a private Christian school, where they looked at her abilities and professional experience when she was appointed. This fact alone is unusual, but a big surprise was waiting for me when I went to visit her and her family. At the time her son was only about 18 months old. I did not recognise this woman. It was like there was a completely different person was stood in front of me. Ines was now married to an ordinary official who works in one of the courts, and there was not much left of her old character.

I had no idea how she could suddenly be so content in herself, calm, relaxed, friendly and accommodating. Ines was living a simple life with no computer or mobile phone. Initially I suspected that this change in her behaviour was caused by living in the country and the sense of community at her church. But everything became clear to me once Ines told me that she had turned to Jesus. She had become a completely new person who had been changed by Jesus.

In 1997, when I needed someone to be a godparent for our son Fabian, I asked her if she wanted to take on this job. Whilst she hesitated to start with, she did then agree to do this. This is why we also have a connection to each other through our families. As I've already mentioned, all of my acquaintances, friends and relatives are non-believers, and so there was only a very limited choice of potential godparents. In the years that followed our families only met up sporadically and not very often. One day Ines told me that her husband was suffering from depression and that he was in hospital. This news hit us hard at the time, because we like him a lot. He is a good person, although his character is far too weak. My friend's family went through some very bad times then, but they kept getting back on their feet. We only saw each other rarely in the years that followed, because Ines did not visit her parents in Saxony-Anhalt very often and we didn't go to Bavaria either. But we spoke on the phone regularly and so I found out that her husband was struggling with increasingly frequent depressive episodes and eventually he even left the family. Even back then I could feel that things were not quite right. But there was nothing I could do. During one phone call in 2013, Ines happened to mention that she had come down with multiple sclerosis. This revelation hit me like a slap in the face. I was speechless and at the time I just had no idea how I was supposed to react to this news. Ines is still a proud individual today. She does not want any sympathy or for anyone to feel sorry for her. That is why she only talks about her illness on rare occasions. I visited her for the first time in years at the start of 2014. I was shocked when she opened her front door, even though I already knew that she could only get about with a walking frame. In terms of her appearance, the woman who was now stood in front of me barely looked like the person I used to know. When she talks about herself, she says that this illness is tearing her apart. This is probably the best way to describe it. Ines has been suffering from this disease since she was 24 and God alone knows how tough things have been for her over the last few years. But she has never given up and she found new strength through Jesus. He has supported her thorugh all of her difficulties, which even means that she has at least been able to work as a teacher for a few more years. Today Ines says that she would have died several years ago without Jesus standing by her side. There has been so much damage to her brain that the doctors who are treating her are surprised that she is atill alive. But she is a fighter and will not allow herself to be beaten. For the whole time I was there, Ines did not come across even once as being sad or frustrated about her fate, but was still trying to see the positive in everything. We chatted for hours and I was able to see with my own eyes how content and grateful someone who has devoted their life to Jesus can be. When I told her how sad it made me feel to see her having to live like this, she seemed very surprised when she replied that she couldn't understand me. Her life would have never been as good as it had been ever since she became a follower of Jesus. For a healthy person this is hard to understand, but it seems that even people with terminal diseases can find fulfilment in life through Jesus.

Ines now lives in sheltered accommodation in a home, after her husband left her a few months ago with their son. Even though my friend was abandoned by her husband, I can still understand that it is very difficult for someone who suffers from depression to cope with his wife continuing to deteriorate. His illness has turned him into a very weak human being. The same thing applies to their son, who just can't cope with his mother becoming increasingly ill and his father's depressive episodes. This means that he is not even capable of holding down a normal job. His confidence is totally under-developped and he has no self-esteem. Their son has not yet been able to graduate from school. It's equally unlikely that he will be able to complete a vocational training course, because he has never learnt to persevere for any length of time. Ines used to be the most important person in the family. She organised everything and made all of the decisions. Her relationship with her husband's parents broke down years ago, because she didn't want to accept their lifestyle any more. At the start there still were some discussions, but as her husband couldn't get his way, contact with her in-laws stopped completely. This story about her family is a complete disaster and so I can understand why Ines always gets very bitter and unhappy whenever she thinks about her relatives or talks about her mother-in-law. This also applies to her own family, because she barely has any contact with her brothers or with her mother. However, God does not want to have people who are unable to forgive by his side. That's why I think that it will be better for my friend if she enters heaven as someone who has been ill, because God could then understand her behaviour. Ines says that she does not need her relatives and so she does not want to see them either. But every time she speaks her voice is full of hatred and bitterness. She is already looking forward to life in the hereafter without any sickness or wasting away. But I think that Ines will only be with God if He takes the illness that is damaging her brain into account. Without this impairment she would have no chance of ever being saved and receiving eternal life with God. How can that be the case, with her having been a really very devout Christian for many years following her conversion?

One of the books where you can find the answer to this question is in "Driven by Eternity" by John Bevere. The author is merciless in his description of what will happen to people who have not turned to God during their lifetime. But he also emphasises that those people who have already converted and so have been free of sin will rightfully be rejected by God if they have later consciously surrendered to sin again. After all, they knew what they were doing. And the mistake Ines has made is that she has disregarded what Jesus told us is the most important commandment, which is to love everyone and to make our peace with anyone you have wronged. She is so bitter, because she is unable and unwilling to forget things that happened a long time ago. But hatred is also one of the deadly sins. And anyone who is full of this emotion will be unable to enter the Kingdom of Heaven. After all, Jesus did take away all of our sins. He set us free from our guilt, and so it should not be that difficult to overcome feelings of hatred and to reach out to our enemies. There are even Christians who have sincerely forgiven someone who murdered their own child or another member of their family. This is totally impossible without help from Jesus. We are so caught up in our own feelings that we cannot find a way out. But Jesus can relieve us of this burden. I hope that Ines still realises how much she has been blessed herself. Perhaps one day she will be able to forgive both her husband, who abandoned her and did not look after her, and also her mother-in-law. I really wish that she does this, because only foregiveness really sets you free. Then of course it's even better if both parties can reconcile their differences. But as we cannot affect the other party's thoughts and feelings very much, we have to be willing to show foregiveness first of all. If someone has done something very bad to us and we have been arguing with them about his for years, then the other person is usually not even that bothered any more. It can even be the case that they have just stopped thinking about this awkward situation at all. But this feeling of hatred eats away at us inside our minds, because we keep on brooding about what the other person did to us. For Ines I really wish that she could make peace with her relatives ones day. Otherwise I hope with all of my heart that God will still accept her as she is, because this terrible disease really does mean that she is not thinking straight.

Andrea looks for a place at a kindergarten

Andrea was from Romania and came to my office, because the school where she wanted to take a language course had suggested that she should get in touch with me. Her son was five at that time and was supposed to be going to nursery for a few more months, before he started school in the summer of 2013. The are never any free kindergarten spaces in Magdeburg and there is a waiting list of several month for anyone who wants to get their child into one of these establishments. There is actually a page on the Internet, which is supposed to show where all of the free spaces are. But in practice it seems that these have already been allocated whenever anyone gets in contact with the institution concerned. In this case I didn't think she stood a chance either, because there is nothing I can do about this situation. Andrea told me in passing that she most wanted to get her boy into the "Mandala" kindergarten, because it wasn't too far away from where she was having her language lessons. Even though I knew better, I made an inquiry at the Youth Welfare Office and of course the answer I got was that the situation was hopeless. However, a few weeks later, one of the people who worked there rang me back to tell me that a space at the "Mandala" kindergarten had just become free. Normally I wouldn't have even bothered calling the Youth Welfare Office, because I know that no spaces can be allocated if there aren't any available. But the fact that I did this anyway is already very surprising by itself. And what are the odds that in such a big city as Magdeburg, where there are 81 children's daycare centres according to the phone book, a space becomes free at that very moment in the one kindergarten the mum had asked for? Mathematically the probability is virtually zero. But by this point in time, the whole situation didn't really surprise me any more, because there are things happening every day, which are given to me by the Holy Spirit. I think it's worth mentioning this case, because it is a typical example that shows how God can get involved and help us out in our lives. Perhaps Andrea will one day remember all of the situations that turned out positively for her, even though there was no obvious solution to them from a purely human point of view. And then hopefully she will wonder whether all of these actually happened by chance and recognise that at the end of the day it was God who helped her achieve this goal, despite the difficulties she was facing. This was not easy at all, because her husband had left her and her child alone in Germany and had gone back to Romania. She had always been dependent on him financially, because he had been working in our country as a doctor and she was not working at the time. God gets involved to help people, even if they are not ready for Him. As it is not important to Him when or where things happen, this aspect is not a factor for Him. The Lord can create connections that extend over a period of several decades. Andrea will certainly not be worrying that much about her faith today. God allows Himself plenty of time and knows precisely when the right moment has arrived and this young woman can also be put on the right track. Miracles like this happen every day, but only those people who have already found their belief in God can see our Creator intervening actively in what happens to us.

At the start of 2015 I got a call from a woman at the health department, who asked me if I knew anybody who speaks Romanian. She had a young woman with her who couldn't speak German yet, but who had an appointment at the state women's hospital, as she was due to give birth very soon. I sent an e-mail round to my contacts on the Internet, but the only replies I got were negative. Nobody knew anyone who was able to help on a voluntary basis and also spoke Romanian. The problem was solved for me when I got a call from the adult education centre one day. On the other end there was a woman I know personally, because our sons used to play football in the same team. She told me the following story. Her line manager was ill on the day I sent the e-mail around, so she got to read my e-mail. She did not react, because she couldn't help me either. A few days later, the adult education centre was taking potential applicants on a tour around the city. One of the people on this tour was a pensioner who happened to mention that she had lived in Romania for a few years. My acquaintance remembered my e-mail straight away, so she asked the old lady if she would be prepared to help the young, pregnant woman. She was happy to pass on her phone number and I called the older woman the next day. During the conversation she told me that she used to work as a midwife and of course she would be happy to help. Several miracles occurred in this story. If the line manager hadn't been ill, then my friend would not even have read the e-mail. She was leading the tour herself and as a result she was the only person who met the old lady who speaks Romanian. If she hadn't known me personally, she might not have bothered reading the e-mail. This is normal in the social sector, because our inboxes fill up constantly. And then the old lady's previous job was just what was needed in this situation. When I told this story to the woman at the health department, she could hardly believe it, but she was incredibly pleased and grateful. This is how God is at work in people's lives every day, but unfortunately many people do not realise how He is providing us with guidance and help, because they do not believe in miracles from God and divine providence. As far as they are concerned, these are all lucky coincidences.

The Miller brothers need help

Alex and Vladimir Miller came to Germany from Kazakhstan at the start of 2014. Their father has lived here with his second family for years, but he would not have been able to resolve the initial problems these two boys had to cope with by himself. The three of them came to our office, because their father wanted the boys to apply for their own flat at the job centre. At that time I still had not quite realised that up to then they had not resolved a single one of their issues themselves, so the boys had not received any money for weeks. I still wonder today how the family could survive this financially. When Alex and Vladimir arrived in Magdeburg and wanted temporary accommodation in a residential home, the people who worked there told them that there weren't any free spaces. They were also not offered any other alternative, which meant that their father had to let his sons sleep in his living room for months. What also made this very difficult was that there is a disabled child in the family who has to be woken up very early every morning, because the bus that takes the children to a special institution in another town leaves at about 6 a.m. There was also another son of kindergarten age living in the family. The only reason there were not any major arguments is probably because everyone involved has a very calm personality. I nearly blew my top when I became aware that I had to start from scratch. It was impossible to explain the situation the boys were in to my colleagues at the job centre. If everything had gone to plan, then Alex and Vladimir would have stayed in this residential home for several weeks and would then have moved into a flat. However, this led to an insurmountable problem. Because the father and stepmother of the two young men are also unemployed, the law says that the two youngsters have to stay with their father's family in a shared flat. But if they had moved into a residential home as soon as they entered the country, which is what is normally supposed to happen, then they would have been legally entitled to their own flat automatically.

So now their father was supposed to find a flat for six people and take in the boys for the next few years. As I've already said, there was no solution to this problem. One day, we had all met up again at the job centre, to try and get things moving and to get some clarity. The man at the information desk could only suggest that we joined the queue and to mention this to his colleague again. First of all, we had already spent two hours in the waiting area a few weeks before and secondly I could not imagine that these colleagues of his would be able to offer any solution to this situation. For this reason and following my inner intuition, I took the boys to the area where people who are making an initial application are supposed to go. I did not have any plan in mind and really didn't know what I was supposed to do. Just at the moment we entered the hallway a nice woman I know privately came out of one of the rooms. Completely spontaneously, I said to her, "You're right on cue and you've got to help us." She answered that we were in luck, because her client had not turned up and so she had some time. This acquaintance of mine helped us by approaching her colleague who was responsible for the Miller brothers. She then stopped what she was doing. Normally she would not have been available and our trip to the job centre would have been a complete waste of time. When she saw us, the colleague who was in charge of their case told us immediately that in this situation it was completely impossible for the boys to get their own flat. However, I gave her the name of my colleague at the Social Welfare Office and asked her at least to ring her. This woman needed to explain to the employee at the job centre that it was the City of Magdeburg's fault that these young men had not been offered a place in a residential home after they entered the country. Her answer to this was that she would give her a call, but that this would not have any effect on her decision. After about half an hour the employee at the job centre told us that she would make an exception in this case after all. Somehow I had already been counting on this, because I could feel that the Holy Spirit was already by our side helping us. His actions never involve us starting something and then the final result of the whole process is then negative after all. A lot of people would now say that it's just a coincidence that all of this happened. But to be honest, what are the odds that I just happen to know the one person out of the several hundred people who work at the job centre, who comes out of the closest door at exactly the right time, who then comes right up to me and who also has time to see us, because her own client had not turned up? Stories like this have happened to me frequently with this family, but up to now it has been possible to resolve all of their problems, even if it has sometimes taken a bit longer. But I also know that the story about the flat at least could never have been resolved using normal methods. The Miller brothers will follow their own path and perhaps later on they will remember how difficult it was for them to start their new lives, but that they have also overcome all of these barriers. Later on the boys were making very good progress. After their integration course, they wanted to go to university in Germany and could already speak German very well the last time I met them.

Viktoria becomes a mum

Another case when I was completely dependent on the Lord's mercy occurred in April 2015. One of my colleagues at the AWO's pregnancy counselling service introduced us to a young and heavily pregnant woman from Kenya who was having to deal with an enormous amount of problems. As I was suffering from a heavy cold at the time, I passed the matter on to one of my colleagues. He was later joined by the intern from the other counselling centre, and they pulled out all the stops to clarify Viktoria's residency status and therefore which authority would be dealing with her entitlement to benefits and her health insurance. However, this proved to be a very difficult task to accomplish, because there were gaps in the information the young woman provided about herself and it is possible that some of this was even untrue. She had been registered in Greece after she fled from Kenya and now has a valid residence permit for this country. But some people she knew introduced her to a penniless, German man and they got married in Greece. He promised her a nice life in Germany and so she moved to Magdeburg with him. However, the two of them separated a few months later and to make matters worse, the young woman now became pregnant by another man, although she was unwilling to give his name. Now the authorities that deal with foreigners had to clarify what Viktoria's residency status actually was. If her presence was tolerated, because she is unable to leave the country due to her pregnancy, then she would be treated completely differently to a wife who was separated from a German man but was living in Magdeburg with a residence permit for Greece. Nobody felt that it was their responsibility to make a decision or even that they had the authority to do so. At the time a lot of the staff were still on holiday, which meant that it was impossible for my colleagues to get a final decision from the authorities who were responsible for her as a foreigner.

Fortunately, Viktoria was allowed to stay with one of her friends who was also from Kenya until the child was born. I was told that this friend is a member of a Christian congregation. She would have felt compelled to help immediately, even though she has three children herself. Even so, her husband was apparently not very enthusiastic about the additional responsibility. So the case kept on being passed backwards and forwards, from the Foreigners' Registration Office to the job centre and to the Social Welfare Office. Nobody felt that this was really their responsibility or wanted to make any final decision, because a situation like this can keep on cropping up and so this would also set a precedent, which would have consequences for other women in a similar position in the future. All I heard for weeks was that nothing had changed and that nobody was getting anywhere. Meanwhile the young woman was getting bigger and bigger, because her due date was getting ever closer. So at the end of April I said that I was happy to sort this case out. I knew that the Holy Spirit would open doors for me that would be kept closed for everyone else. I arranged to meet Viktoria one Tuesday first thing in the morning at 8 o'clock outside the Foreigners' Registration Office. Fortunately their offices would not be open for another hour, which meant that I had time to reassess the situation and develop a new strategy. If the Authority had actually opened its doors when we got there, then I would not have been able to achieve anything that day, because I would have had to join the queue with everyone else who was waiting, but I would not have known the member of staff dealing with the issue at the end. They would have sent us away again without a satisfactory outcome. However, I went to the Social Welfare Office with Viktoria, because I wanted to find out which problems might have arisen from the member of staff concerned. This authority also only opened its doors at 9 o'clock, which meant that we joined the queue. I prayed to the Holy Spirit and asked Him to send us a solution. At that moment one of my colleagues from the Social Welfare Office entered the building. I knew her very well from other cases we have been involved in. She recognised me immediately and took me to meet her line manager. I also have a very good and fairly friendly relationship with her. These relationships are worth their weight in gold for people who do my job. She rang the Foreigners' Registration Office for me, to ask them who was dealing with Viktoria's file. Even she was passed around between various members of staff, until it was eventually established exactly who was supposed to be dealing with this case. She told this man that I was already on my way to the Foreigners' Registration Office with the young woman, so that the decision to grant a residence permit or not could finally be reached, after everyone involved had been waiting for this for weeks. If I hadn't had such a good relationship with this colleague from the Social Welfare Office, then no direct contact at all would have been established with the Foreigners' Registration Office. So we went back there. There were a lot of people in the hallway, but I still knocked on the member of staff's door, because I had some other meetings later that day. He told me that he hadn't managed to look at the details of the case and that he still had to read through everything. The employee asked us to come back to see him two days later, because he would then have reached a conclusion. Of course you could now be saying that other migration advisors who were not Christians would have been able to clarify the situation just as easily, so there would be absolutely no proof that the Holy Spirit intervened. And that is precisely the difference between faith and hoping for good luck. Believers can feel when they are being helped actively, whilst other people are just pleased whenever a few lucky coincidences happen at the same time. But the first thing I would then say is that you would not normally expect all of the relevant members of staff to be in the office at the very time when I turn up there unannounced without an appointment. And secondly, not everyone picks up the phone immediately if the office is understaffed because a lot of people are off on holiday, even if they get a call from another office at the city council. What's also interesting is the fact that so many people had tried to tackle the case and weren't able to get anywhere. The Holy Spirit decides when a problem will be solved, we just have to accept that.

At 9 o'clock in the morning two days later I turned up as agreed at the Foreigners' Registration Office with the young woman. My client was then told that her husband would have to support her, as he was only allowed to marry her if he could provide for her. However, up until that time, nobody really knew how this man actually earns his livelihood and how much income he has. He had even neglected to register his wife with the police in Magdeburg. So she was staying here illegally for many months. Fortunately she was never stopped by the police. I was at least able to sort out this problem with her that day and get a registration certificate issued for her. With this proof of her identity she was able to register for health insurance and also with the bank later. In May 2015 her husband disclosed all of his documents, after he had been invited to a meeting at the Foreigners' Registration Office. But even the letter from the lawyer, which asked him to provide information about his income and his wife's health insurance fund, bore fruit. Viktoria now had everything she needed. She was able to register for health insurance, at the job centre and at the bank. It is a borderline miracle that the job centre immediately paid her the money due to her for the child she was expecting. Normally applications like this are not processed anywhere near as quickly. She was offered a flat very quickly and even got approval for this just for herself, because her husband lives on a pension that is far too small for him to be able to provide for his wife. At around the same time a pram and a pushchair were donated to our office, which meant that Viktoria had what she needed for once. I do find all of this a bit surprising, because the member of staff at the Foreigners' Registration Office had clearly told us that she was not entitled to any kind of financial support from the German state. I think that God decided to help the young woman and the new life and so he changed the laws here, which were very clear. There is no other way I can explain all of this. After all, I have never heard of a case where somebody was given money that they were not legally entitled to. The fact that Viktoria's husband gave false information from the start and did not disclose his true income is a different matter. He will definitely have to take responsibility for this one day. Little Abraham was born on 12.05.2015. He is a healthy, strapping boy, who will hopefully bring his mother nothing but happiness. Viktoria also needs contact with other people, so I invited her to visit the congregation when the child is a bit older. I will be careful not to give my opinion on Viktoria, because it's not my place to do that and God will judge everyone in the end anyway. So if she has deliberately provided false information so that she would be able to live in Germany, then we might never find out about this. But we also don't know what fate awaits this young woman. And at least the fact that he is growing up in Germany is a very good thing for the child.

Orlando has an operation

I met Orlando for the first time in December 2013. He had only recently arrived in our country and was totally disorientated. This young man came to my office, because his right foot was so badly injured that he couldn't put his weight on it. So Orlando needed an operation urgently. The biggest problem for both of us was that his understanding of German was practicaly non-existent, but he also did not really make much of an effort to learn it. Portugese is spoken in Guinea Bissau, the country he originally came from. When my colleague from the Social Welfare Office rang me to ask whether I could help him, I answered that I couldn't speak his language either. But I didn't want to just abandon him, because at the time I already had a hunch that he would need a great deal of help from me. So I went to the doctor with him, even though I could not give him much help and we all had this language barrier. Other members of the Network for Migration in Magdeburg gave me the details of a man from Angola who is happy to help out free of charge with small translation jobs. I got in touch with this man a few days before the first visit to the doctor. He was happy to help any fellow human being who needed help, even without anything in return. But at the time, none of us quite realised the saga that lay ahead of us. If any refugee wants to see a doctor, they have to get a treatment certificate from the Social Welfare Office in advance, because these people are not insured directly by the state health insurance funds. The Social Welfare Office settles the medial costs with the doctor who is providing the treatment. Every time he had to make another visit to the doctor, we first had to go to the Social Welfare Office on the other side of the city to get this treatment certificate. The first GP that examined Orlando told him that his foot was already so stiff that nothing more could be done. He would just have to live with the pain.

But she did also give him a letter of referral to a surgeon, so that Orlando could get a second opinion from a specialist. In the meantime I had got hold of the interpreter's mobile number and then got a description of how the accident happened. Orlando had broken a bone in his heel in August 2013 whilst playing football. As this fracture was not treated in Africa, the bones did not fuse back together properly. It was always painful whenever he put his weight on it, which of course meant that he could never walk properly. As a result the joint had frozen almost completley. As we couldn't take up all of the interpreter's time without paying him, I asked the doctor who was treating Orlando to send the diagnosis to his phone and he then translated it over the phone for Orlando. All the surgeon was able to do was confirm that it was too late and the bones had already fused incorrectly. That was actually all he could do in this case. But he did also advise the man to ask for more information at the University Clinic, because the treatment methods they had there were even more advanced. Of course the Social Welfare Office will only pay for complex major surgery of this kind if it is absolutely essential and none of the cheaper treatment methods promise successful results. But before this happens, the public health officer has to assess Orlando and confirm that surgery on the foot cannot be avoided. The young man had to wait about three months for the appointment with the public health officer. During this time he could only hobble around in pain, which is obviously very difficult for a man in his early twenties who was used to playing sport. One day something astonishing happened. Even though I could not have a conversation with Orlando, we could still understand each other. During yet another car journey, I asked him if he believed in Jesus. Even today I still don't know how that could have happened, because most of the people we look after are Muslim. I normally wouldn't ask this question, which is why I believe that God was guiding me at that moment.

Orlando told me that he was a Protestant Christian and so I took him with me to the Sunday service at my church. At the time my daughter was going to confirmation classes every week at the YMCA, the Young Men's Christian Assocation. One of the younger members of staff there told me that there are a number of different youth groups at the same place. There are students in one of the groups who meet every week. This even includes a young man from Brazil, where Portugese is also spoken. I immediately thought of Orlando and that I had to take him to this group, so that he could learn German more quickly with people the same age as him and can have some contact with local people. I went with him to one of the meetings. Immediately afterwards, Orlando told me that these people were completely different from the people he would meet every day in the city. That is not surprising, because they were all friendly to him. At this meeting he could already see that it's good to have Christian friends. Orlando also felt very welcome in the congregation, and the people who met him were all polite. However he only went to the church if I was also there. This is the reason why he later didn't go to the service for weeks and eventually stopped going completely in the end. Orlando still had to become more independent and more confident, because I can't look after him 24 hours a day. But that is exactly what he was not capable of doing. However, it really is a miracle that God kept him safe and picked him out of the mass of refugees. I think that he owes the enormous amount of help and love he was offered and received to his own actions. He prays to the Lord every day and prayers do get answered. After many weeks of waiting and of uncertainty the big day finally came and at the end of March 2014 Orlando was finally allowed to see a consultant at the University Clinic.

There he was told that the most they would be able to do was to strengthen his joint using needles. Whilst he might not be able to have full mobility in his foot then, the pain would probably disappear. This diagnosis was completely the opposite of what the two doctors had previously told him. The waiting was finally over at the start of April 2014 and Orlando was able to have his operation. Everything had gone smoothly up to that point, but now a serious problem cropped up. As we were discussing things at the Clinic, the doctor asked me to bring an interpreter along to the preparations for the surgery, as important information was given then, which had to be translated without fail. Unfortunately at the time I had not realised that the hospital is required to provide an interpreter if the patient does not speak German. That would have saved us a lot of hassle.

When I rang the interpreter to ask if he could help, he did not have anything in his diary and agreed to help. When I called him back shortly before the day when the preparations for the operation would be made, to remind hm about the appointment, he suddenly informed me that he wouldn't be able to help now after all. In his defence I should mention that this man works on a royalty basis and so cannot afford to turn down an offer of work. As a single parent, he also has to provide for his daughter. But I suddenly no longer had an interpreter and did not know what to do. I had no money available for this, which meant that I couldn't just hire another translator. The man from Angola changed his mind when I told him that this was terrible, because I had promised the doctors that I would bring an interpreter along. He rang me back later to tell me that he could actually make it, although he only had two hours free. At the time I really did think this this would be enough time. So the next day we were sat in the preparation area waiting for the doctors to talk to Orlando. The day before I had promised the translator that I would give him 50 Euros of my own money for his selfless act of assistance. The reason for this is that I don't look at the value of money in the same way as most people do. As far as I'm concerned, every Euro is just borrowed from God, so that we can honour Him by making the best of his gifts. It was exactly the same in this case, because as we will see, this gesture affected what the interpreter did later. The time just zoomed by. I suddenly realised that there would be a really big problem if the interpreter had to leave us, because he didn't have any more time. I prayed for God to help us, because I knew that it would take weeks for Orlando to get a new appointment for an operation. The interpreter was getting increasingly agitated as every minute passed and I was getting annoyed with him. Suddenly he said just one sentence, which changed everything: "I have decided to cancel my appointments, because I've realised that my being here is more important. At the end of the day, we're talking about the life of a human being." Initially I was so overwhelmed and grateful that I just couldn't believe it. We kept waiting and in the end we spent five hours at the clinic. After all the waiting around was finally over, the interpreter said the following, "I feel really happy now, because I've done something good." How could that be true, as doing this meant that he had lost money he needed to live on? Most people would not do or say anything like this. I have already heard several people expressing the opinion that this man must have been stupid, because he would not be able to live without any money. Nowadays nobody could afford to help out in a situation like this for free.

After this long morning at the University Clinic I drove the translator to another town, where the second job he had been offered was now already waiting for him. Of course I felt obliged to do this, because he had helped us so much. As we drove I asked him, "Do you know how to recognise a Christian? By the fact that they do things that other people would never do. There aren't very many people who would miss out on earning money just to offer help to somebody they don't even know personally." His answer to this was that he did believe in God, even if he had not been to church for a long time. But he does think that the Creator sees his good deeds and so will not forget him. This attitude is not a bad start, because it can eventually lead to someone finding God and being saved later on. The translator also told me that my actions helped him make his decision. He became aware how much time I had invested by that point in trying to help Orlando and that I had also given him money for translating. When I said that I was just doing my job, he replied that people can work in different ways. He didn't know any other social workers who were so committed to their clients. I was not anywhere near as good a person before. It is possible that it would not have mattered to me at all, if the preparations for the operation had all come to nothing and Orlando had had to wait even longer. I would have just dismissed it as "one of those things we can't do anything about it." As I've mentioned, today my feelings and thoughts are completely different. When I first visited the hospital, I took my friend Walli with me. She was one of the tutors I knew from the church. This old lady does not have any family and so she was happy that somebody was paying her some attention. This also gave her the feeling of being important and being needed. Orlando showed how pleased he was by calling us Grandma and Mum.

Even the doctor who was treating him thought it was strange that someone from Africa was talking about his German mum. I thought this was nice, because it shows that he trusted me. He was discharged from the hospital one Tuesday. It later became apparent that this was exactly the right day, because the authorities and the doctors surgeries had longer opening hours that day. This meant that we were able to get the treatment certificate we needed for his GP at the Social Welfare Office and even register him at the practice too.

Another interesting point is that I was on holiday the day he was discharged. When I went with an old lady, whom I will tell you more about later, to visit Orlando in the hospital, we were told by the staff there that he had already been discharged. I wondered what I should do next. My first thought was to drive back home again. But then I got a feeling that he needed my help. And that's exactly what he needed. There were so many things to sort out, which we gradually worked our way through. I finally invited him and Waltraud to a small restaurant for coffee and ice cream. The waiter was very surprised when the three of us walked into the bar in the village. Spending time together was important both for Orlando and also for Waltraud. At the end of the day I also went shopping for some food for the young man, which I paid for, because of course he had nothing in any more at his residential home. That day was followed by a few more visits to the doctor, the Social Welfare Office and the physiotherapist, but on 11.06.2014 Orlando found out that his treatment was then over and he had to learn how to start using his foot again in future using targeted exercises. Today he can dance and ride a bike again, which is what I am most pleased about, because it shows that perseverance often does help people achieve their goals. After he had been living in Germany for one and a half years, he got the news that his application for asylum had been rejected. As he had never taken my advice to heart and had not learnt German, the situation became very difficult for him. The members of his family were waiting for him to send money home every month, even though this is actually intended for him to support himself. This is a common practice, especially amongst refugees from Africa. Our government knows that these people don't just use this support to pay their own bills, they also send a large chunk of it back home. However, they tolerate this situation, because it supports the members of their families in Africa indirectly. Child mortality has gone down, which is one positive result of this policy. On the other hand the family members become dependent on Europe and stop working their farms. This means that the land turns back into desert and normal life is no longer possible in these countries. I really do wonder if this is a good thing. It would be better if the industrialised countries and especially the people who hold the pursestrings supported the people on the ground by setting up a viable infrastructure and businesses and providing work and opportunities for them to earn money there. But global politics, which we will never really understand, are to blame for the fact that this does not work for the most part. Unfortunately many refugees from Africa have only been to school for a few years and so they cannot meet the entry requirements for a vocational training course. Orlando did go to a school in his country and in theory he should have been able to complete it. But he was too fragile, which is why he did not accept the help he was offered on more than one occasion. He would have been able to learn German from the AWO and make friends with members of the Protestant community. I was able to show him the options that were available to him, but in the end he had to take the initiative himself. When he goes back to Guinea Bissau at least he will be able to us all his strength when he starts working there, because he is now healthy again. So it was right for him to have this operation in Germany. A few months later, one of his compatriots from Guinea Bissau told me that Orlando had gone to Portugal, because his family is now living there and he wasn't getting on very well here. Despite his lack of flexibility and his immature behaviour, Orlando has something that has brought him success, his faith in God. As a Christian, he never doubted that God would help him. This trust in God has earnt him his salvation.

Maria, a confident, young woman

Maria comes from Syria and lives in a traditional family, one in which a woman still has a lower social status than a man. But at least she did not need to keep her head covered and was allowed to move freely around the town up until 7 o'clock in the evening without being accompanied or supervised by a man. By 2014 she had been in Germany for two years and could speak German very well. After a year on a vocational foundation course she got her school leaving certificate in July 2014 at the end of the academic year. I realised immediately that this girl was very active and was quite capable of making her own decisions. She had a goal in mind and was happy to accept any difficulties this caused. Maria had probably been to every advice centre there is in our city to speak to an advisor, because she desperately wanted to start training to become a specialist medical assistant in the summer of 2014. She even found herself a doctor's surgery where she could get some initial work experience.

In contrast to her, the way her twin brother has been brought up has had a very negative influence on him. Up until June 2014 he would never even talk to me, because I had once told him off about his inappropriate behaviour towards other young people. That did not fit in with his view of the world at all, as in his opinion women are not allowed to make the rules and always need men to help them. However God works in mysterious ways and so he turned up at my office again a few months later, because he needed some help. Before I turned to God I would have sent this young man away, because he was very arrogant and demanding. He used to moan about everyone. I was always very uncomfortable with people like this. To be honest that's because I still don't understand to this day why someone who has had to flee from their country now complains about everything in the place where they are safe. I am surpised at how calm I stayed during this conversation. Basically he was also just a poor, little lamb trapped in the rigid structure of his extended family. The boy always wanted to talk down to his sister and to this day he probably still can't understand that she has been more successful than him. Many months later I had a very revealing conversation with his brother Hafez, when he told me that years ago this boy had been in a coma for several months. At the time nobody believed that he would ever wake up again. But he has had this difficult personality since then. They did not like to talk about this matter very much, because it was uncomfortable for them. However knowing this was very important for me, because I could now finally understand that this boy did not have anything against me personally, but he did generally have major problems. But I still don't know how he could ever cope in our society. Nobody will have any sympathy if he exhibits such stubborn behaviour as this. The advice I had always given to Maria was not to allow herself to be influenced by anyone and to find her own path. She told me why it was so incredibly important for her to get a place on a training programme. If she did not start learning a career, then her father would have arranged a marriage for her. In families like this it is not the usual practice for 18-year-old girls to still be living with their parents. Either they go out to work, which is probably only tolerated in European countries, or they just get married. When I asked her if she had at least met the man she was supposed to be marrying, her answer was no. Maria might have been a very progressive young woman, but she was also trapped in her own culture and religion. Of course she did not want to break off contact with her family, even if she disliked this kind of life. As she had fled to Germany with her family from Iraq and their application for asylum was still being checked, it was very unlikely at that time that she would get a place on a training programme. Basically the Foreigners' Registration Office has to grant permission to start a vocational training programme or take up employment whilst the assessment was being made and if the application for asylum happened to be rejected. And getting consent for this always depends on the individual member of staff. At the time she was not able to apply for financial support or a training grant from the state either, because she did not have a residence permit. However during her school work experience, the doctor was so impressed with her that he suddenly decided to offer her a place as a trainee. But Maria definitely needed the permission of the Foreigners' Registration Office before she could do this vocational training. So in May 2014 I sent a letter of recommendation to the authority and gave a detailed explanation as to why she should be given permission. Of course I did not say anything about the marriage, because things like this are always kept quiet. Just under two weeks later the young woman came to my office and asked me if I had already received an answer. In the meantime she had become totally desperate and said that she would kill herself if it didn't work out. This gives you an indication of how awful this situation actually is for these girls. Of course I talked it over with her and told her that she shouldn't lose hope. There is always a way out, even if that's hard to believe right now. She went home, but then turned up again shortly afterwards with a smile on her face and the authorisation in her hand. She started her training in the summer of 2014. Exactly a year later she moved to Hamburg where her fiancé lives, but I was assured that she would be continuing her training there. I really hope this works out for her sake, because otherwise she will never be independent.

Hafez is allowed to continue his education

In May of the same year Maria's big brother Hafez also came to see me. He had already been studying economics for a few years in Syria and wanted to continue his studies in Germany. Unfortunately refugees who are already going through asylum procedure are not allowed to do this, because they don't get any kind of financial support for this from our state. He was extremely frustrated, because he had already been sat around for months in the home for asylum seekers with nothing to do. As far as Hafez was concerned, I was his last hope. I wanted to support this young man from the start, because I realised how seriously he was taking his situation. Getting ahead in life has always been important for him. He did not just want to take, he also wanted to achieve something. I thought to myself that perhaps he could do a vocational training course at least, even if he wasn't allowed to go to university. In my opinion, his knowledge of German, which was self-taught, was not good enough for him to study at university anyway. He agreed with all of this. I looked for some information on the Internet and found out that a vocational college in our city was offering a course where you could train to become a commercial assistant. I registered the young man there and they were very happy to take him, because he already had some prior knowledge of this subject. In August I had a meeting with the principal and some of the members of staff at the vocational college where they told me that unfortunately they would not be able to ofter this school-based vocational training course after all, because not enough people had registered to take the course. However, in the meantime Hafez had been given permission to start a vocational training course by the Foreigners' Registration Office, even though he still did not have a residence permit. I prayed to God and asked him to find a solution to this problem and especially for the young man. During this meeting I told the principal that I was surprised that another private college was offering exactly the same commercial assistant's training course. But as the colleges were not talking to each other, the other college could not run this class either and twenty or more young people would be kicking their heels on the street at a stroke. A miracle happened a few weeks later. The state vocational college was sending all of the applicants who had registered to start training to become a commercial assistant to the private college. Nothing like this had ever happened before, but anything is possible with God's help. Hafez got his residency permit in 2015 and is now studying economics at university.

Elvis gets a chance

The following events happened exactly one year later. Elvis, a young man from Kosovo, came to see me in my office and told me a strange story. He was born in Magdeburg, because his parents had come to Germany as refugees from the civil war in the 1990s. They were sent back home once the war was over. He studied criminology there. But when he showed the officials at the crime office his documents and they noticed that he was born in Magdeburg, he could not get a job after he graduated. These people are not considered to be refugees in their own country. Instead they are regarded as traitors to their country, because they left their homeland in the most difficult times and did not fight for freedom in their own country. Elvis cannot do anything about this situation, because he was born much later and nothing he could do would affect the situation at all. He has now been back in Magdeburg since the start of 2015 and also did not want to go back to Kosovo. He was living in a single room at the residential home for refugees. The likelihood of his application for asylum being granted was very low from the start. One day he was sat in his room feeling dejected and pretty depressed, with no prospects and without any confidence. Suddenly he heard someone putting a key in the door to his room and trying to open it. The person who was trying to get in was surprised to find out that there was already someone new living in this room. It was Hafez of all people, who had gone back to where he had been living to pick up a few things he had forgotten when he moved out. The men started talking and Elvis told him about his hopeless situation. Hafez then suggested to him that he should get in touch with me, because I had helped him too. Elvis did go to the first few years of school here and so can speak German perfectly.

So much for the background to this story. The first thing I did was to get Elvis a place on a training course at the same private college where Hafez had spent a year completing his school-based training. The principal, who is someone I know well personally, was happy to take him, as he had been to take Hafez the previous year, and arranged a grant for this training from a European fund to support the disadvantaged. He could see how motivated these young people were. There was no way they would drop out of this training course, because they would then be at risk of being kicked out of Germany and deported back to their country of origin. The young men were also very grateful, because we were giving them a chance by extending a helping hand. Despite this, the Foreigners' Registration Office refused to grant him permission to start the vocational training course, because Elvis still needed to find an apprenticeship where he would be paid enough during his training to stop him continuing to be dependent on support from the state. Eventually he found himself a place with a painting and decorating company. Elvis still had to travel back to Kosovo, so that he could enter Germany again with the aim of starting a vocational training course, because this meant that he had a different reason for coming to Germany. But he was now not dependent on support from the state and can even apply for German citizenship after eight years if he wants to. This example should make us realise that people who are really in need are even willing to get qualifications for jobs that are lower than their level of education. Perhaps he might even start a course at the Police College later, once he has German citizenship, as this was one of the admission requirements. They would have loved to take him, because up to now there have not been many young people from a foreign background who have shown an interest in policing as a career. And these people have the benefit of knowing the language. Up until then he will learn that working as a painter and decorator can also be satisfying and more than anything it will give him security.

A few days after that another young man from Iraq came to my office. He had also been sent there by a colleague at the Social Welfare Office. He had also been sent back home with his family a few years earlier, once the war there was over. He speaks very good German and English, which is why he got a job working for Lufthansa in his home country immediately. People there do not need to have any specific vocational training. It is enough for them to be able to speak several languages. This young man had now left Iraq again, because he had got married and was not earning enough to support his family. He had also got a place on the training course at the school I mentioned before, because he was motivated and could speak German perfectly. Without the prospect of this, it is possible that he would have been forced to leave the country again, along with his wife and child. We might disagree as to whether it makes sense for young people to leave their countries of origin and come to Germany to live, even though they are not being persecuted there. But perhaps it makes more sense to use the skills they bring with them. Of course these young people realise that it is worth fighting for their own interests. Whilst the solutions are provided by God's miracles at the end of the day, the youngsters may find out that they are surrounded by people who have their best interests at heart and want to help them. It always takes a very long time for people's perspectives to change anyway. I just hope all of these people will still find their way to God as well. Their culture and upbringing are a big influence on them, so you can't just beat them into submission by talking to them like a teacher. The most this will achieve is that they refuse to listen. In some cases I do actually understand their attitudes towards values and norms. For example, Maria does not like the fact that some youngsters in our country are so disrespectful in how they treat each other. I have a good idea of how things would have gone on some days at the vocational training college. Some young people have no idea at all how to talk to other people in a friendly way. And if some of the girls wear very revealing clothes, that certainly doesn't help very much when the young men are then expected to show some respect. Maria finds this all very shocking and so she would never go to a club. I can completely understand that she is worried about this kind of behaviour. But of course I have also made it clear to her that not all young people behave in an inconsiderate or selfish way. There are people everywhere who do not want to adhere to social norms and their behaviour always reflects this. As I mentioned before, on the other hand, she hates the way her father decides things for her and basically treats her like his property. He says that he wants to protect her from these youngsters, but in doing this he stops her making any decisions of her own. This example shows us very clearly that young people from foreign countries in particular are often torn apart in their personal attitudes, because they do not know how they are supposed to live their lives. The young men from Muslim countries don't have things any easier either, because they are bound by their family's code of honour. They can't break out of these structures, if they don't want to lose their whole family and their circle of friends at the same time.

I have spoken with young people from Syria and very often they just don't like these constraints that are imposed on them. They want to take their opportunity and make something out of their lives. Some of them manage to do this, they do an apprenticeship and realise that this gains them respect and acceptance in German society. And then time and time again there are setbacks too. Young people who were heading in the right direction, but are then forced to drop out due to circumstances in their families. I was totally schocked when I found out that one young man I had been dealing with and who also wanted to start a vocational training course had stabbed and killed the father of a Syrian family and so ended up in a prison for young offenders. Incidents of knife crime like this always involve honour and unfortunately they also usually involve illegal financial transactions. This youngster has lived in our country with his family for years. It does make you wonder what went wrong in his upbringing for something so awful to happen. I think the worst thing about all of this is that the mothers in these families are not able to take enough care to all of the children they have and so don't give them enough love. As most of these marriages are arranged, there is often no loving relationship between the husband and wife. If anything, in some cases the women even have to share their husband with several women. If a child is growing up in an atmosphere like this, then in the end he or she will barely be aware of emotions. I can see no other explanation for why I have to spend hours telling some of these youngsters how important it is to lead a meaningful life. Finally someone is listening to them and is giving them the undivided attention they deserve. Many young people from Muslim families are not at all familiar with things like personal conversations. The young man, who now had to serve his sentence in a prison for young offenders, was already very conspicuous when he was still at school. But as far as I'm concerned, the fact that the boy committed this crime with so much brutality and callousness is absolutely incomprehensible. I am certain that he will not have been reformed in prison. I am not saying that all Muslims are being brought up like this, but I have seen that boys in particular are simply missing out on love from their mothers in their childhood. It is sometimes really depressing, but also gratifying how receptive these young men are towards me, once we get to know each other better. Their fathers bring them up to be men who are not allowed to show any kind of feelings. But even these young human beings feel joy, pain and suffering. So where are they supposed to go with these feelings? I have a great deal of sympathy with everyone who is trapped in their own religion or culture and is not able to develop freely.

Rosi wants to be treated fairly

I find this story particularly moving, because it shows that children and the elderly often have no voice in Germany. That's why we have to stand up for these people. In particularly hopeless situations I often get the feeling that God wants to put me to the test there and then. I heard Rosi's painful story for the first time in November 2013. My spontaneous reaction was that I wanted to help her right away. Rosi is just over 80 years old. I have known her for more than 20 years, because she is a friend of one of my relatives. We did not meet regularly in the past, but we have often bumped into each other at family celebrations. Her relationship with her two children can't have been particularly good, because she has never said anything about them in all these years. At the start of 2013 Rosi was still living alone in a small flat. She was not very well at that time. She was mentally confused, mainly because she was taking a large number of tablets and she was in the early stages of dementia. As a result her children arranged for her to be hospitalised. Her physical and mental condition improved noticeably due to the medication she was prescribed and administered there. In my opinion she would have been capable of managing in her own home when she was discharged, if she had some help from her children. But they had no interest of any kind in helping their mother and arranged a place in an old people's home whilst she was still in hospital, which meant that Rosi was then taken straight there. Her own children did not inform their mother that they wanted to take on the power of attorney for her or that she would be living in a home in the future. They drove Rosi to this old people's home, disappeared without saying goodbye and left their own mother behind as if she was someone they hardly knew and as if they weren't bothered what happened to her. Rosi was faced with a fait accompli. She had to share a twin room with a woman who was bedridden and who called the nurses several times a night. I try not to imagine what this awful situation was like for her emotions. How does this affect someone who can recognise these circumstances in their own environment very well? Rosi was initially put into a closed section for people suffering from dementia, which basically meant that she was shut in this small room and the adjacent hallway. Her children were not the slightest bit interested in this at the time. I can only assume that their mother's welfare was not important to them, because there was no sign of them for the first few months and they never called. Luckily Rosi had a friend at the time who looked after her and who came to visit her regularly, otherwise she would probably still be in this predicament today. I never got the impression that her own children made many more plans for her. They thought that she would be safely shut away in this home and would never be able to leave it again. An observant nurse then arranged for Rosi to be moved into another room, because that section was actually completely the wrong place for her.

When I got involved and first of all sent a letter both to the district court and also to the Social Welfare Office, she had already been put into a room with another woman, who was suffering from depression but otherwise kept herself to herself. Rosi now had her own TV, but she could only turn it on if her roommate agreed. As this woman always went to bed early, Rosi would end up having a short day. What's more, Rosi had not liked the food from the start and of course living in such a confined space was not easy for her. In other words, her situation was still unsatisfactory. What I wanted to achieve with my intervention was for the people who worked at the Social Welfare Office and at the court to exert some influence on her legal representatives. The children should be making sure that Rosi gets her own room and has access to her own accounts. The first issue was suddenly resolved surprisingly quickly, but nothing else happened at all after that. It was incredibly important for this old woman to know how much money she had. It might sound a bit strange, but as a child who had been a refugee after the war, she had learnt to save every penny, because she had had to work hard for it. Rosi has maintained this basic attitude for the whole of her life. She is still a very frugal person today. If you look at things from this perspective, you can understand Rosi wanted control of her own property. Her children were only the administrators of her assets and so it should not have actually been hard for them to show their mother her savings books and the bank statemtents for her accounts once a month. And because they absolutely refused to do this, I was of course very sceptical the whole time and suspected that they were stealing money from my friend's accounts. It bothers me immensely that family members have unrestricted authority over their parents, if they are classified as suffering from dementia at an advanced age. Old people don't have any way of getting themselves out of this position. They need someone to support them in their efforts. In Rosi's case this meant that her daughter in particular became ruder, more insolent and more disrespectful in her behaviour towards her mother from one occasion to the next, because she was convinced that she couldn't do anything about this patronising attitude anyway. Nobody who was involved in Rosi's case at the time was willing to accept reality and do anything about the situation for my friend. Rosi had told her daughter several times that she did not want to live in this home. Of coure there are much better and nicer residential home for the elderly, although these are much more expensive. But as I mentioned before, my friend could certainly have afforded this luxury, because she had been saving for her whole life. Having her own children telling her how to spend her money is, in my opinion, not legal. That's why we got into a dispute with the authorities.

All of the decisions that the judge dealing with the case made were based on the doctor's diagnosis that was made in July 2013. In my opinion, however, up until May 2015 Rosi was not any more confused than most people of her age. I have no idea how many letters I ended up sending to the court asking them to finally take the requests my friend was making seriously. In June 2014, after six months and without any further explanation, the judge dealing with the case decided not to consider or reject the application Rosi had made for a change of caregiver at the end of April. Rosi never received any written notification from the court about the rejection of her application. I had said I was prepared to acts as her legal representative. It's not as if this was something I particularly wanted to do, because it would also entail extra unpaid work for me. But I could not bear the thought of horrible way that Rosi was being treated any more. So I also contacted the Higher State Court in Naumburg and later the State Court in Magdeburg to lodge an appeal against the decision of the Mental Health Court in Magdeburg and I also complained about the actions of the judge who had been dealing with the case. On both occasions my letter was sent back to the competent District Court, because it is not within their purview to deal with complaints there. But this did result in the case being dealt with at least. At the end of June 2014 I also filed a criminal complaint against her children with the police on behalf of my friend, as they had withdrawn money from her accounts without permission. This case was passed on to the State Prosecutor's Office, as access to the accounts can only be granted if consent for this is given by the legal representative, which in this case meant the people who were being accused. Clearly anyone can see that this would never have happened. At the end of August 2014 I had an interesting conversation with the judge at the Mental Health Court, when he told me that with everything I was doing I should consider the fact that my friend was suffering from dementia and so would not be a credible witness. Even while we were still discussing this, it became clear to me that I could not expect any help from this quarter. However the judge dealing with the case did visit my friend personally in the old people's home a week later and afterwards appointed someone from the state to administer her affairs. As this person did not contact Rosi in their first month in this role, I wrote to this judge again. I told him that the situation my friend was in had not changed.

As I expected, there was no reaction and so at the start of November 2014 I finally instructed a lawyer to investigate the situation. He then applied to the Mental Health Court for access to the files, which he was eventually granted after weeks of waiting. When these were looked at, it turned out Rosi's children had been asked to present the accounts to the court in the middle of 2014. They did not comply with this request and the judge who was dealing with the case simply did not pursue this matter any further. So at the end of August, when he told me that a detailed audit of the finances had been carried out, which did not show up any anomalies, he was deliberately not telling the truth. That automatically begs the question why someone who represents the law can take such a cavalier approach to rules and regulations. I suspect that there is tacit acceptance nowadays that some of our fellow citizens who are driven by greed will get rich from their parent's property as soon as they are declared to be legally incapable. At the start of January 2015 I gave the lawyer a list of the accounts and saving bonds along with their balances in May 2013. This allowed him to finally hold the District Court accountable and to have the abuse uncovered, as the differences could now be proven. From the start, it was the job of the administrator who was appointed by the court at the end of September 2014 to reassure everyone involved, but otherwise he was not meant to make any changes. This was supposed to stop my friend saying anything, but this was not possible, because in spite of everything, for a very long time she continued making the same demands as she had when the actions started in November 2013. Whilst the children have not had any access to their mother's accounts since September 2014, it was obviously still impossible to work out the final total of her assets. At the end of March, so two months after the lawyer had asked the District Court to repopen the case, I notified the State Court about the lack of action by the judge dealing with the case, because I had a suspicion that he had never intended to find out the whole truth about how much money had been misappropriated. If that was the case, he basically would have had to admit that he had been deliberately deceived, but did not take any action against this offence. As the State Court is not responsible for these cases, the matter was redirected back to the executive committee in charge of the District Court again. This had the advantage that nobody was now able to get out of their responsibility to review the matter or continue to delay the process any more. But even the judge presiding over the executive committe informed me in a letter on 21.04.2015 that there had been no irregularities in this case. When I read this I wrote back to him again and told him that as a committed Christian I cannot tolerate the behaviour of the court. I condemn any kind of injustice and dishonest behaviour. It is obvious that I was in the right, because the executive committee of the District Court did not defend itself against my accusations and just did not react.

Unfortunately my friend's mental condition deteriorated so much after May 2015 that she was no longer interested in her money and stopped fighting for justice for herself. Whilst her children are no longer her legal representatives, they will still inherit everything one day anyway and nobody will ever hold them to account for their behaviour. This whole story is still very strange, because my acquaintance was initially declared mentally incapable by a recognised doctor, but then she was still allowed to appoint her own lawyer. This fact shows that the old lady was overlooked, because people with dementia are no longer able to say they want to have access to their own accounts. It is a sad and disgraceful state of affairs that an old person was treated like this, when she is still able to go shopping at this time and can look after herself, because the court, the authorities, the residential home and even her own children had conspired against the victim. Today I know that Rosi is not an isolated case. Again and again children use money belonging to their parents to line their own pockets, after they have been declared to be unable to function. They don't even need to list all of the accounts in court, as the judge is unable to check whether ths information that has been presented is correct. The children can then calmly start spending the money they would inhert once their mother dies anyway. This case also shows that people affected by dementia can do absolutely nothing in these circumstances. As soon as the court has declared them to be incapable, their relatives have free rein to do what they want. In the Bible we are told that "pride come before a fall". If her children and the judge at the Mental Health Court had only come a bit closer to responding to Rosi's wishes, then these major problems would never have arisen. The family drifting so far apart is also due to the fact that Rosi's husband and their father died young and this was never discussed at the time or dealt with in terms of their emotions. This is probably the reason for the extremely cold hearts of everyone involved. Perhaps they can all still experience healing through Jesus. This is my great hope. But it is also very important to me that those people who worked on this case are also able to realise the truth before it gets too late so that they can be saved. Time is running out.

Natsnet and her husband Habtom

In June 2016 a young man from Eritrea came to see me in my office. He was looking for a flat in Magdeburg for his sister (Later on it turned out that they aren't related to each other at all) and her baby. At that time it was still possible to provide migrants with somewhere to live. In October 2015 I had started arranging shared accommodation for the large number of young men who had mainly come to Germany alone and with no family after September 2015. Each and every one of them was of course entitled to their own flat by law, but the law often bears no relation to the real world. After many of them had formed groups and moved into shared flats with each other, the space for accommodation that was still available became more and more scarce. Today in 2018 it is almost impossible to find a flat that is still free. I particularly wanted to support Natsnet because she had a baby she had to look after. So I told her friend which documents the landlord needed to issue a tenancy agreement. Three months went by and nothing was happening. When the suffering is great enough, even the last of us are stirred into action. Natsnet was living in Thüringia, but after 01.08.2016, so two months after her friend first got in contact with me, the law requiring recognised refugees to be given housing was changed. Before that date, any migrant who had been given a residence permit for Germany and was still living on welfare payments was able to move to a town of their choice. This led to a situation where these young men in particular were moving to towns all over Germany. This meant that officials were hopelessly overwhelmed by the administration of their files and the associated changes. This is the main reason why the requirement to provide accommodation was amended on the first of August 2016. Since then any migrant who wants to move to another federal state must have relatives there or prove that they already have a job there. This rule was tightened up once more, because since 17.02.2017 refugees who are given a residence permit from that date onwards also can no longer leave the administrative district they have been sent to whilst they are still dependent on welfare payments.

In Natsnet's case, this meant that she was not actually allowed to move to Magdeburg any more, even though she had to move out of her flat in Thuringia in September 2016, and so now finally started getting things together. Somehow she then very quickly managed to get hold of all of the paperwork I needed that I had been waiting three months for her to find. In the meantime I had almost forgotten the young woman, but fortunately I had not been able to find a tenant for the flat in Magdeburg by then. It is too big for a single person and to small for a group of people. Shortly after the young woman had arrived in Magdeburg with her child and its father, she received a letter from the Foreigners' Registration Office telling her that she had to go back to Thuringia immediately. Fortunately I was able to explain to my colleagues there how important it was for the young woman to stay in Magdeburg. And of course it was also helpful that I had already applied to the job centre in Magdeburg for her to be assessed for a flat in July, which meant that this authority had already given its consent for this in July 2016. At the time I prayed for his young woman a great deal, because I realised that she was absolutely helpless and could not manage anything by herself. The first problem arose when she went to register with the police at the Citizen's Office. There they realised that the baby only had a temporary residence permit so far, as its application for asylum was still being assessed.

It is not actually the case that every baby born to a refugee in Germany automatically gets a residence permit, even if both parents already have one. Each refugee has to be assessed individually by the Federal Office, as one day they will all be adults and will then no longer be dependent on their parents. As it just had this temporary residence permit, the baby was not allowed to leave Thuringia. When I objected to this, as the baby could not possibly live on its own, they had to check the law. So the mother was allowed to move to Magdeburg, but not the baby. The next time we went to the Citizens's Office we showed them the baby's birth cretificate. This was then accepted, because there is no residence requirement on this. Then I had to explain to Natsnet that her husband Habtom was not allowed to move to Magdeburg, because he still did not have a residence permit at that time. He had come to Germany later and the two of them had only met here in Thuringia. As it later turned out, the young woman, who had given birth in February, had not managed to apply for child benefit or the allowance for raising a child in Thuringia before September. So I had to work closely with the authorities in Thuringia, which took a lot of time and was very complicated. But in the end I was able to persuade the Foreigners' Registration Office that staying in Magdeburg would be better for Natsnet. I don't know what her life was like in Thuringia, but none of her applications had been completed there. This was the first hurdle we had to clear. But it then took a while before she was able to start getting any welfare payments, because she told the members of staff at the job centre that he was her husband when she turned up for her first meeting there along with the child's father. As far as she is concerned that's what he is, because they got married in church here in Germany. But they are not a married couple under German law, because they don't have a legal marriage certificate from a registry office. But they can't get married, because neither of them entered Germany with a passport from Eritrea. This created a bit of a dilemma, because Eritrea doesn't have passports according to my clients and the Eritrean Embassy in Berlin does not issue travel documents for their compatriots. I had to explain to the members of staff at the job centre several times that Habtom just couldn't move to Magdeburg due to the restrictions on where he was allowed to live, because the law says that he has to stay in Thüringia, and that the two of them are not married in the eyes of the law. At some point even this problem was resolved. After he finished his language course in Thuringia, the young man obviously wanted to move to be with his family in Magdeburg. Natsnet was never able to go to German lessons, because she fell pregnant soon after she started living in Germany.

In May 2017 I went to the registry office in Magdeburg with her and Habtom to apply for him to have his paternity recognised. This is because the young man can only move to Magdeburg if he can prove that he is the father of the child or if he has found a job. He was not recognised as the father, because they are parents without the right documentation, so they cannot prove their identity. However the Foreigners' Registration Office can only grant permission for him to move after his paternity has been clearly confirmed. The only way to do this is to have a blood test, but this is not exactly cheap. And then it turned out that the young woman was expecting her second child in January 2018. By some miracle she got a place with a childminder for her first child in September 2017. I had applied to the Youth Welfare Office for a daycare place for her, even though I knew that there are no free spaces anywhere in the city. I think that she got this place because she lives near the childminder. Of course this really was a stroke of luck, as her child was only a year and seven months old when she got this place. They had to act quickly, so that Natsnet could at least go to German classes between September 2017 and January 2018. There was also a local course starting close by in her neighbourhood, which meant that she had enough time to get from the childminder to the language classes. In the meantime it was clear that the Foreigners' Registration Office would not grant her husband permission to move unless they had a positive paternity test. That was also when a colleague from the advisory service for migrants came to my office and gave me the address of a cleaning company that, according to his information, is always looking for staff. I went to this company with the child's father and it turned out that in fact they had just started looking for a new member of staff. Whilst this was a temporary contract up until the end of October, it was a way for him to get started on the job market. The company was very happy with his work, which meant that they then offered him contracts for more temporary work. He is still working for this company today. As the young woman had not managed to apply for parental allowance in Thuringia and they didn't get all of the documents they needed until much later, she did not get this paid until months later. At the start of 2017 around 1,200 Euros was paid directly into Natsnet's account as parental allowance. She had no idea where the money came from and spent all of it. Months later, when the job centre in Magdeburg demanded this money back, she just did not have it any more and couldn't get hold of that kind of money. As a result, Natsnet was then asked to start paying her own rent for the next few months. As the young woman had not understood this letter either, she ended up with massive arrears on her rent. This even led to her getting her rental agreement terminated without notice and she was asked to vacate the flat. But in the end even this situation got sorted out, as I was able to arrange a standing order for her so that 250 Euros a month would be transferred from her account. After a phone call with the relevant member of staff at the job centre, they agreed to start paying her rent again. The rent was no longer in arrears by the end of November 2017. This came at exactly the right time, as the young parents then needed more money again, because their second child was about to arrive.

Of course with all of these things you could put them down to coincidences and timings working out perfectly, but I still say that things like that don't just happen. It all worked out so well, because God was directing us. For example, there were some problems with the childminder, because her doorbell was not working and Natsnet did not have a mobile. The other mothers were able to ring and let her know that they were there. But two days in a row she was left standing outside the door unable to get in and thought that neither she nor her child were wanted. In the evening I got a WhatsApp message about what happened. We ended up in a group chat with the childminder, who cleared everything up. At the end the childminder told me that she would now check whether Natsnet was waiting at the door every day at the same time. I got another call on 17.10.2017. I was told that the child was ill and so could not be left with the childminder. I told the mother to take her child straight to the paediatrician. I went to meet her, but she never arrived. She had forgotten where the doctor's surgery is, even though we had been there several times. As I was just about to start walking towards her flat, because I assumed that she must have gone home, I met her on the footpath. I'm mentioning this incident, because I just don't believe in coincidences like this. In November 2017 the family applied to move into a bigger flat, as there would definitely not be enough space for four people to live in a two-room flat after January. However, even today the property company they had rented this flat from is still inflexible and uncompromising in how they approach things like this, because the tenancy agreement was fixed until December 2018. They are not even prepared to offer the family the three-room flat two floors up in the same building, which is currently standing empty. Their justification for this decision is that the three-room flat would be overcrowded with four people. This suggests that the people who work there are obviously forgetting that in Magdeburg it's quite normal for families with two children to live in a three-room flat. And what's more their two-rooom flat is already really overcrowded as it is. I think that they could have come to an agreement if they had really wanted to. The family had to learnt to cope with this new situation, even if it was a step into the unkown for them and also a bit of a challenge. The husband goes to work and the wife takes the older child to the kindergarten. With the strange situation that the Foreigners' Registration Office is not allowing the father of the two children to move from Thuringia to Magdeburg and the family is not allowed to move out of their flat, they now have quite a lot of money. This is because the husband's earnings cannot be deducted from the benefits Natsnet receives from the job centre for herself and the two children. Officially they are not considered to be cohabiting, unless the Foreigners' Registration Office confirms this officially. There is a reason for everything and perhaps in future this will be the family I use as an example of successful integration. I have told this story in so much detail, because I wanted to show how many coincidences had to occur in this family alone to resolve all of the issues they faced. People who do not believe in God would say that I just have good networking skills and always know the right official to talk in each department. Whilst I do agree with that, often the timings work out so perfectly that everything can just fall into place as we work though the case. And that is the main reason why, with my Christian faith, I do not believe in coincidences, but in God's providence.

Walli needs help

Christians who have turned to God and received the Holy Spirit behave differently to other people. I can see this most easily in myself. Today I do things that would have been unthinkable for me before. My friend Walli is a good example of this. When I went to the service at the Baptist Church for the first few times in 2011, one particular elderly lady stood out. Walli had been a primary school teacher in her working life and so has still not got rid of her "commanding voice" even today. At the time I thought, "Hopefully I will never have to talk to this person. That is bound to be extremely stressful." But everyone knows that God always works in ways that we are not expecting. When the church started offering schoolchildren help with their homework in the afternoons, I said I was happy to help. At the time I wasn't actually a member of the congregation, but I thought that perhaps one day my clients could also benefit from this help. And so I thought it was only fair for me to do my bit. Of course doing this I was bound to meet Walli, because she was a qualified teacher as I mentioned and this was a welcome change for her as a pensioner. Back then I was only working half days, which meant that I had time to get involved on a voluntary basis. Initially I avoided the old lady who was still driving herself around at the time. But one day she asked me for my help. Her computer was not working properly and so I went back to her house with her. There were photos of two young men hanging on her wall. When I asked her who these men were, she replied that they were her children. One of her sons died from a hereditary disease at the age of 24 and the other one died when he was 45. I was shocked but also impressed, especially because this woman never lost her zest for life, despite these personal setbacks and always remained confident if not even cheerful about her life. In my opinion the only way this can succeed is if Jesus gives us inner peace.

This experience led to a fundamental change in my attitude towards life. Even today, Walli is still a great role model for me as far as this is concerned. Over the next few years we met more and more frequently and also did a few things together. In May 2017 I even went to a Christian youth meeting with her. The young people were delighted to have her there, because she is up for any kind of excitement. However, Walli is not a person you can mess around, because she immediately goes on the defensive if she realizes that someone is patronising her or trying to make her do something she does not want to do. This is the main reason why nobody wants to look after her. She was suffering from dementia, which started deteriorating quickly at the start of October 2017, especially after she fell several times. Since then she cannot live alone in her flat any more, because she cannot use her hands for the simplest of tasks. I asked Jesus to give me the right words whenever I spoke to her, because I knew that she would shut down immediately if she noticed that I might be trying to tell her what to do. For her to agree immediately to my offer of becoming her legal representative or guardian was even more astonishing for me. This would make it easier to find a place in a care home for her. It normally takes months for an old person to get an appointment to assess the degree of care they need. But it's not very easy to get in a good old people's home without proof that you need long-term care, because it's impossible to finance this on just a pension. I spent days scratching my head, trying to work out how to get around this problem, because I could see that my friend's physical and mental condition was rapidly getting worse. At the start of October she spent a day in the University Hospital. But the doctor treating her discharged her again immediately, because patients cannot be kept in a clinic against their will. Walli left the hospital at her own request. But in this confused state she could not live alone in her flat any more.

On 15.10.2017 I found Walli in a totally despondent mental state in her flat when I went to pick her up at 9.30 in the morning for the service. The Holy Spirit had already urgd me to hurry that morning, which meant that I got to where she lived much earlier than usual. It was a good job I did, because it meant that we had enough time to get to the church eventually and still arrive on schedule for the service. At the time she was not able to walk very well, because a few days earlier she had had a fall in her flat and injured herself. I took her along to the service, even though she kept on falling asleep there and could not concentrate any more. The reason I did this was because I knew that I would meet her GP there. She had a better understanding than me of what had to be done now. At that moment it was clear to me that Walli could not go back to her flat. The next time this happened she might not be able to get out of bed any more and would no longer be able to open the door. Fortunately the doctor advised me to take Walli to a hospital that specialises in cases like this. It was the right decision, because they took really good care of her there. The doctor who admitted her was nice and friendly and showed real empathy for Walli and understood what was going on. In other words, I was absolutely delighted, because I knew that Walli was now in good hands. Once again God's timing was perfect, because it meant that the process of applying for the assessment of the level of care she needed would be much shorter. At exactly the same time I also got the answer from the District Court to the application for me to become her legal representative, which Walli had been pushing for a few days earlier. This letter was lying there opened in her kitchen. I took it with me the day Walli was admitted to the hospital and gave it to the doctor straight away, so that the hospital could get in contact with the court without any delay and so the application could be processed more quickly. This was very important, as the process from the initial application until legal representation is granted usually takes several months. When I discussed this with a colleague a few days later, she told me that there was till space free in a twin room at the AWO's care home. So I then got in contact with the home. After her stay in hospital, my friend had to go into short-term care, which meant that she was looked after in the home for a month. It is a legal requirement that anyone who is in short-term care has to be assessed by the health insurance medical service during this period, to determine whether they can still live alone in their own house.

The medical service sent someone to the carehome on 16.11.2017. My friend's care was assessed at level three, because she has other physical disabilities in addition to the early stages of dementia. This was already absolutely wonderful, but the fact that a single room she could move into also became free immediately was even more impressive. These rooms are like gold dust. She is now very happy in the home, because the residents get round the clock care. She is also a sociable person who needs contact with other people. They organise activities there nearly every day, which she joins in with regularly. She had to give notice on her flat so she would officially move out in December 2017. The notice period was three months. This meant that I had enough time to clear the flat in peace. But having to pay two lots of rent meant that my friend's bank balance was pushed to the limit. I could not hire a company to clear the flat, because Walli could not afford this. So I started clearing the flat in the middle of December, with help from some refugees from Eritrea. They needed furniture for the flats they had just moved into and some of Walli's cupboards were still in good condition. Some unusual things happened that were actually very helpful. Walli had around ten crates of drinks in her flat. Some of these were full of bottles that were already past their expiry date. One say, when I was already wondering how I could get rid of these crates, I met a man in the hallway who was pushing a trolley loaded with empty crates. I asked him if he could take Walli's crates as well, which he was happy to do. I told him to keep the money he got back for the empties. This helped us both. Of course you could just say that my bumping into him was a coincidence, but that's not how I see it. Then when I was wondering how I would get rid of all the rubbish and furniture that was in the flat, I found a brochure about the city providing free refuse collection in her letterbox. Was that good timing, a coincidence or just help from God? A short time later, another one of my acquaintances told me that he had taken the old furniture that belonged to his aunt to a charity shop. She had also gone into an old people's home then. They give the items to socially disadvantaged people for a small contribution. I then gave them a call and at the start of February 2018 the charity shop sent people to collect the furniture that the migrants didn't want, and exactly two days later I arranged for the items that could not be reused any more to be taken away as bulky waste by one of the waste disposal companies the city uses. There was also an example of perfect timing here, although the date for the rubbish collection is only announced a few days in advance, i.e. there could have been weeks between the two collections. I also took a lot of things to the dump myself. It took three whole months until everything was gone, because I could only do an hour at a time and I was doing everything by myself.

I sometimes wondered why I did so much for Walli, especially as she is just one of the many people I know. There was also the issue that she could not understand why I gave her furniture away for free. She didn't need the money and it helped other people. The interesting thing about this is that even Christians often do not want to give their possessions away to poorer people. Walli's son had previously made a lot of donations to charitable organisations. I got upset a few times when she accused me of not demanding money for her furniture. But then one of the people who worked at the care home spoke to me, which reassured me again. She explained to me that old people like to hang on to the things from their past, even though they don't need all these possessions. And the caregivers who look after the residents of the home the most also feel the most pressure, because these elderly people complain to them about everything. Of course I understood this already, but hearing these words helped me immensely. On 20.02.2018 the judge from the guardianship court spoke to Walli and asked her if she wanted me to be her legal representative. And yet again it was explicitly pointed out to her that she only has to stay in the home if that's what she wants herself. Now, one year later, the conclusion I can draw is totally positive. This is because everything that has happened over the last year has been the best thing that could have happened to my friend. She is very well looked after in the care home. The geriatric nurses work really hard to make sure that she is always well. There is no way of avoiding the fact that there is still some friction occasionally, because Walli can be very stubborn and her dementia has now reached a very advanced stage. Sometimes she now even has difficulties recognising the days of the week. But Sunday is always the highlight of her week. Then I pick her up for the service and she gets to meet other people. Time and time again the staff at the old people's home are always amazed that I keep going with this so regularly. But I think to myself that one day perhaps someone or other might recognise that God's love conquers everything, because this story has now allowed me to build up a very friendly and open relationship with all of the staff there. You could say that they can see what it means to love your neighbour. And as far as the story with Rosi is concerned, I came to the realisation that at the time the court probably reached a different conclusion before she was admitted into an old people's home because a doctor had certified her to be suffering from dementia and not able to live in her flat alone any more. There is no other way I can explain the situation, because I an one hundred per cent sure that she never wanted to live in a home. So a doctor and the wishes of her own children were dictating how she lived her life. It is frightening that people can sometimes have such a negative influence. But in my case, I am pleased that I became the legal representative for both Swetlana and Walli, as this also allowed me to find out things that I would never have come into contact with otherwise.

My emotional and spiritual awareness has expanded, because I have been able to find out what people have to do when they work in the care sector in the workshop for the disabled or at the old people's home. This time, as I was able to experience at first hand what the process for getting an old person admitted into a care home is like, I was even more shocked by the way my other friend Rosi had been treated by her own children three years before. Rosi's dementia had not advanced as far as Walli's when she had to be admitted into the home. This is also the reason why her children had not applied for her level of care to be assessed at the time. The assessor from the medical service specifically asks the old person several times if they want to stay in the home or go back to their own house. I am one hundred per cent sure that Rosi's answer then would have been no, because her children did not ask her or even let her know that she would be spending the rest of her life in a home. At that stage, her mental condition would have meant she could have stayed in her own house. They would have only had to apply for home visits from a nurse. But what is even worse is the fact that Rosi was actually put into the closed unit for dementia sufferers at the old people's home by her own children. Even today I am still not sure how they managed to arrange for the daughter to become her legal representative, even though the guardianship court checks very carefully whether the old people have signed the declaration of consent. All of this is very sad, but if the relationships in the family have broken down do much that there is no longer any emotional connection, then there is nothing else you can do as an outsider. It is interesting that a lot of people ask why I am so committed to helping people who aren't even related to me. They just cannot imagine that there are people who only do things because of their love for other people and not because of greed. But that is exactly how you can recognise devout Christians. They become more and more like Jesus, because that is what He wants.

The reaction to my posts on the Internet

I am convinced that we human beings are in the End Times, as they are described in the Bible. Many of the things that are happening in global politics today are exactly the same as what the prophets and Jesus predicted. I have not gone looking specifically for websites on the Internet that deal with what are know as "conspiracy theories". But one day I came across a post that aroused my interest. This included facts that answered some of my questions, because there has been a radical change in the political climate in Europe since September 2015. And suddenly everything that was happening in the world no longer appeared as logical. My work became more varied and my Facebook statuses became more comprehensive after I studied the various posts. The Holy Spirit gradually gave me insights into the meaning of the Islamic religion and how the world we live in is structured. As always, I published the things I had learnt on the Internet on Facebook, because I wanted everyone else to find out the truth as well. However, this has led to me being attacked since then by some people who are Christians in name only and have formed a group that sees it as their duty to expose everyone who considers themselves to be someone who follows "conspiracy theories". In a democracy it must be possible for different opinions to be tolerated, even if they are not the same as mine. But that is the problem that these people have. They do not want to accept or even consider the possibility that the things I talk about on the Internet might actually exist. I don't agree with everything that other people think either, but I would never come up with the idea of condemning them. But that is exactly what these people have done. They sent messages to my employer that were supposed to expose me as a "right-wing fanatic". But I have only passed on facts that can be proven on the Internet. However, I get the impression that criticism of the political situation is often seen as inappropriate or even undesirable. Up to now in my professional experience I have almost exclusively met Muslim people who are just as peaceful as most German people. That is why I would never claim that all Muslims are prepared to use violence and want to change the way our society is organised so that it matches their views. The only wish most Muslims have is to live in peace and to be recognised as an equally-valued member of this society. As a converted Christian I am quite capable of differentiating between the religion of Islam as such and its followers, some of whom have only started following this faith because of the fact they they were born in a Muslim country where Islam is the state religion. However, these Christians I have mentioned see things differently. Because they are of the opinion that someone who has a critical attitude towards Islam must also automatically have a negative attitude towards Muslims, they see it as their duty to force me to lose my job and so destroy my livelihood. I will absolutely not allow myself to judge the behaviour of these people, as they are actually convinced that they are doing the right thing. They want to protect refugees and fight right-wing extremism. That is very commendable, but must happen in the right context. I hope that they recognise their mistake one day and will realise that they would have ruined the live of a fellow human being, if the Holy Spirit had not held his protective hand over me. Deliberately causing someone harm, no matter what the reasons are, is not Christian. Hopefully these people will recognise that soon. I do not condemn them because of their behaviour, as I know that these people have been blinded. However this story has also made it clear to me that as Christains we must trust and obey God unconditionally, if we want to stay afloat in this world. In July 2016 I was given a warning by my employer, which stated that I would be dismissed immediately if I kept on publishing critical posts on the Internet. The people who were throwing accusations at me had not just contacted my employer, but also the press. But they weren't interested in someone like me. This obviously made my accusers very angry, because they tried again exactly one year and three months later. Fortunately by that point my warning had already lapsed, as otherwise I would not have stood a chance. I would have lost my job immediately. It is still a mystery to me today how the Lord has managed to keep me away from them for so long.

The second attack followed in September 2017. They complained to my employer and some of the other authorities again about someone like me spreading "extreme right-wing views" on the Internet. Of course my boss was not happy about this situation, because she could not understand that I kept on putting up critical posts, even though the difficult position I am in had to be clear to me. A rational person who is not being led by the Holy Spirit would not have done this either. When asked why I continued putting up posts on Facebook that were not necessarily in line with public opinion, despite being aware that this was clearly a very complicated situation, I simply answered that I had my own opinions. However, after this incident I reached a compromise and renamed my old account on Facebook. At the same time I created a new account, on which I wrote less critical posts for the next few months. I know that I would never have got throught this situation without the support of the Holy Spirit. My friend Johaness told me that all of these things are examples of Satan's hostility and that I have to defend myself against them. In my mind, I already understood this, but my body was telling me that by this stage it would be pure madness and it would ruin me if I kept on doing this. This internal conflict really was on my mind a lot. I kept on praying to the Holy Spirit, asking Him to show me what I should do and whether my posts were actually telling the truth. I asked Him to stop me spreading lies if that's what they were. In the past what actually always happened was that I culd not write things that were not correct. I was at the service on 17.07.2016 and I got a message that could not have been clearer. This day became a turning point for my whole life. The pastor said in his sermon that we should not be lukewarm Christians, who start something but don't finish it. Of course, even though he was directing his words to everyone, I got the feeling he was speaking to me personally. On the very same day I started publishing the rest of what I had come to realise. So I put myself one hundred per cent in the hands of the Holy Spirit and stopped just trusting my own more rational mind, which was telling me I was being stupid, as I was risking my own livelihood by doing this sort of thing. God wants me to pass on this information and to obey Him. I know that He would never get me to do something that would ruin me. And as I have been allowed to have so many so positive experiences with Jesus over the last few years, I finally stepped out of my own shadow, overcame my fears and did God's will.

Some people might now be saying that I have been very lucky in my life and that the only reason many of my problems have been solved was because I have a positive attitude about life and over the years I have been able to build up relationships that are very helpful for me in my professional activity. That is true and I don't deny it either. But how I feel personally, since I had my conversion, is something only I can feel. I used to behave completely differently before in my relationships with my fellow human beings, which is something many people who knew me back then can also confirm. But they are not surprised by how I behave today in many situations. My friends, family and other people who know me do also wonder how I got all this knowledge about my faith. It really is true that the

Holy Spirit shows anyone who becomes a Christian what they need to know. I also admit that I am still not a studious reader of the Bible and I also don't stick to all of the laws in the Bible one hundred per cent. An awful lot of devout Christians post on the Internet that it is very important to follow all of these laws. I don't dispute that, but if this becomes the focal point of my life, then I am no different to the Pharisees from the time of Jesus. Of course we have to point out how important it is to follow Jesus. But if all we do is continuously threaten other people with a wagging finger and tell them off, we won't achieve anything at all. Nobody wants to be lectured all the time. In my opinion it is more important to use our own personal example and actions to show how God wants converted Christians to behave. We should show our inner calm by being in a good mood and friendly to everyone. And everyone should see us like this every day. This is almost always the case with me. In fact I do have the inner calm I need for my job, my friends and my family. My colleagues say that I am totally relaxed. I agree with this one hundred per cent. Although I was also very fortunate in my previous life, which, as I've mentioned already, is something I don't just put down to my own abilities.

I talk very openly about the new things I have experienced and I'm passing them on now, because I want to encourage some of the readers of this book to reconsider their beliefs. The main thing I want to do when I'm recounting the stories about the migrants is to show that my experiences with them have usually been good. This is incredibly important, because currently we just tend to see rather negative reports about refugees in the media. Of course I do realise that there are black sheeps in every community and in some there are perhaps even a few more. But basically condemning someone, just because they are members of one particular religion, is something I believe to be wrong. It is shocking, how some people on the Internet, who even describe themselves officially as Christians, openly spread hatred against Muslims or Jews. This makes them just as dangerous and guilty as those people who use terrorist attacks to raise the political temperature in Europe. But we should be able to criticise the behaviour of certain people, irrespective of their religion. Because if it is no longer possible to object to something that goes against our own moral code, then I have no idea where this path might lead us. I know that I will not reach everyone with my stories. Perhaps some people might even find it amusing and poke fun at someone like me who makes things like this public. That does not bother me, because Christians are always the target of hositility anyway. It is particularly important for me to say that I don't believe that Christians are better people. Nobody gets preferential treatment from God, not even the Jews. The only reason they are God's chosen people is because the Lord uses them to show how He acts. And everything He has said about this nation of people has been fulfilled one hundred per cent. As this applies to all of the prophecies in the Bible, I am sure that what it says about the End Times will also come true. As far as we humans are generally concerned, we should know that it is high time we repented. God is waiting for everyone to take this step! As you can see from my story, we do get some gifts whilst we are still on Earth. But our motivation should be the desire to become reconciled with God again. This is because where we will be spending our eternal life is so immensely important. You still have time, but from a human point of view it is very short and could be over at any moment! Anyone who finally wants to find inner peace that allows you to look to with future with optimism should very carefully reconsider the idea of turning back to God again.